John Wesley Bookwalter

Siberia and Central Asia

John Wesley Bookwalter

Siberia and Central Asia

ISBN/EAN: 9783743316522

Manufactured in Europe, USA, Canada, Australia, Japa

Cover: Foto ©ninafisch / pixelio.de

Manufactured and distributed by brebook publishing software (www.brebook.com)

John Wesley Bookwalter

Siberia and Central Asia

SIBERIA
AND CENTRAL ASIA

BY
JOHN W. BOOKWALTER

*ILLUSTRATED FROM PHOTOGRAPHS TAKEN
BY THE AUTHOR*

Springfield, Ohio
1899

PREFACE

This book is the result of a trip through Siberia and Central Asia, made by the author during the summer and autumn of last year. It consists mostly of letters written by him while on the journey, which were published by several Western newspapers.

Owing to the great and increasing importance of the Eastern Question, the author has thought that it might be of interest to his friends to have these letters put into a more permanent form, illustrated by many views taken by him at that time. These views in themselves may, perhaps, be his best excuse for the book, as they give a better and clearer idea of these great regions than any words of his can convey.

As the Eastern Question hinges largely upon the position of Russia, the author undertook this trip for the purpose of studying that country at short range; and, owing to exceptional privileges granted to him, he has been led to think that the results of his observations there may serve as a contribution to the better understanding of that question. He has, therefore, issued this book for private circulation, and asks the indulgence of his readers for a work thrown off during the excitement and fatigue of a long journey in new and most interesting lands.

J. W. B.

SPRINGFIELD, OHIO, *April*, 1899.

CONTENTS

CHAPTER I
PAGE

Trans-Siberian railway—Its commercial and political importance—The effect it has already produced—Russia's military strength—Napoleon's estimate of Russian soldiers—Probable international complications to arise from Russia's industrial advance eastward—Our own relation thereto—General features of the Trans-Siberian railway—The trains and their equipment—Travel on the post-routes of Russia—Humane law respecting horses 1

CHAPTER II

The Russian steppes—Their similarity to the prairies and plains of the United States—The lands of Russia—Geological division of the same—The great Tschernoziom lands of Russia—Their capacity and products—System of farming in Russia—The yearly production of cereals—Exports of same—Russian live stock and export statistics—Manufacturing and mining industries—Culture of Indian corn—Population of Russia—Distribution of same—The rural and urban population of Russia—Dwellings and other buildings in the villages 18

CHAPTER III

Emancipation of the serfs—Peasants now great land-owners—Emancipation rescript of Alexander II., in 1861—Condition of the serfs prior to this act—General provisions of emancipation rescript—Obligatory redemption of lands—Measures to facilitate same—Distribution and allotment of lands to the serfs—Division of serfs into three categories—Effects of emancipation act—Its tendency to lessen conflict between capital and labor—Devotion of the peasant to his lot acquired by this act—An impediment to emigration to Siberia and other distant lands—Russia's position in the probable clash of nations—Number of serfs liberated under the emancipation act—Date of the proclamation—The peaceful accomplishment of this great act—Peace rescript of the present Czar—Is Russia rightly understood by other nations? . 32

CHAPTER IV

Stations and restaurants on Siberian Railway—Equipment and safety of road—Syzran on the Volga River—The Tartar—Bridge on Siberian railway over the Volga River—The Volga, its size and importance as a highway—First view of the Ural Mountains—Their height, etc.—The city of Zlatoust—Government works and mines in the Ural Mountains—Summit of the Urals— Entrance into Siberia—Some facts concerning the Russian Empire—Eastern slope of the Ural Mountains—Crop conditions in the Volga Valley—A look ahead 43

CHAPTER V

The Asiatic continent—A glance at Siberia, its geography, physical characteristics, etc.—The great rivers of Siberia—Erroneous impression of Siberia—Vast area of level land—No difficulty in construction of railway—Similarity of Western Siberia to a great portion of the United States—The error of Americans respecting trans-Missouri River country—The route of the Siberian Railway—Its construction and equipment—Stations on railway in Siberia—Track, bridges, etc.—Accumulated grain on the route from

CONTENTS

Kurgan to Tomsk—The necessity for increased facilities on Siberian Railway—Flora and fauna of Siberia—Agricultural resources of Siberia—Possibilities of the country . 73

CHAPTER VI

Ultimate Siberian railway system—Proposed line from Central Siberia to the Persian Gulf—New relations between Russia and China, arising from the Siberian Railway—Change from route as originally projected—New route to Vladivostok—Rapid settlement of country on Siberian Railway—Quick growth of towns on the line—Development of lands to follow railway extension—Grazing lands on Siberian Railway —Small lakes through Siberia—Timber in Western Siberia. 103

CHAPTER VII

Kurgan on the Tobol River—The Kirghiz Tartars—Their tents, villages, mode of life, etc.—The future of Kurgan—Winters in Siberia—No blizzards in Western Siberia—Rainfall—Petropavlovsk on the Ishim River—Rapid change in country on railway line—Emigrant trains eastward—Growth of grains on the line of railway—Surplus awaiting shipment—Omsk on the Irtish and Om rivers—Interesting character—Tomsk on the Tom River—The prison in Tomsk—Flourishing college—Electric lights, telephone system, and other conveniences—Condition of railroad east of Tomsk—Various excursions from Tomsk into the country . . . 123

CHAPTER VIII

Travelling on post and common roads in Russia and Siberia—Unique outfit—Splendor of private equipages—A Siberian tarantass—Manner of hitching the horses—Speed discomforts and excitement of travel on tarantass—Seeing Tartar life in its simplicity—A queer-looking vehicle—Homely but effective—Experience versus philosophy—Furious driving—

CONTENTS

PAGE

The village sheik—A compatriot of the great Circassian, Schemyl—A Mohammedan—His family life—Beauty and filial devotion of his children—His wives—Influence of the wife among the Kalmucks—Kirghiz village—Hospitality of our host—Our Yamstchik—His style and skill as a driver—Great speed of horses without use of whip—Return to Tomsk—Various modes of travel 152

CHAPTER IX

Return westward—Route across the Kirghiz steppes to the Caspian Sea—Down the Volga River to Astrakhan—Rise and commercial importance of that city—Modern trade diversion and its effects—Russia a land of fairs—Nijni Novgorod and its great fair—Kharkov, Ilinsk, and other leading fairs—Preferred route across the Caspian Sea to Central Asia—Importance of the Volga River as a means of transportation—Numerous fleets of coal-oil barges—Statistics of freight traffic on the Volga and Onega system—Partiality of Russians for American products and methods 192

CHAPTER X

Development of Siberian agricultural resources—Its effect upon similar interests in other countries—Prime conditions governing the future reclamation of lands in Siberia—Waterways of Russia—Careful development of same—River system in Siberia—Severity of winters restrict their use—Season of navigation—Omsk as a centre of a vast cereal region—Its possible connections by water and rail with foreign countries—Necessity for greater transportation facilities in Western Siberia—New route being created from Omsk to the Baltic—New route between Russia and Western Siberia—From Omsk to Havre or London—Comparative distances 212

CHAPTER XI

Transportation route in Southwestern Siberia—Route between Caspian and Black seas—To connect the Volga and Don rivers—All-waterway between Caspian Sea and Europe—Neglect of American waterways—Careful preservation of same in Europe—Methods of utilizing rivers in Europe for transportation purposes—Use of the Seine in France—Through the heart of France in a boat—Neglect and decay of American rivers as lines of transport—Railways versus water transportation—What would result from thorough development of American river system—Russia's real progress—Great foresight—Not doomed to the fate of China—Russia in the field of diplomacy—The official class—Redundant population—Its danger to all nations—Unwisdom of developing urban at the expense of the rural population—Results in the necessity for land-grabbing—Wise policy underlying settlement of Siberia—Plan of settlement—Conserving old vested interests—Deterrent influences in settlement of Siberia—Rapid growth of population—Its current necessities—Probable effect of Siberia upon markets in other countries 224

CHAPTER XII

Russian life in Siberia—Visiting various villages—Siberian towns and villages—Mostly frame or log houses—Efforts at ornamentation—Number and appointment of rooms—Clothing of the natives—The Icon—The Russian peasant most religious—In the peasant's home—A mark of respect never to be omitted—Custom of recognizing the Icon in Russia universal—Fare of the peasant—A singular bathroom—The drink of the peasant—Two kinds of quass—Vodka, its use and effects—Salutary regulations by the government—Worthy of imitation by other nations—Siberia the land of the exile—Erroneous impression of the traveller—Courtesy of Russian officials—Abolition of serfdom—Its effects contrasted with abolition of slavery in America—Administration of justice—Respect for law and authority—Difficulties encountered by Russia in its development—Obstacles to its progress—Remarkable national development—Banishment of bank officials to Siberia—Their status during and after term of sentence—Punished for fraud at gaming—Not a good country for irregular practices—Passport system—Citizens of Russia required to have passport—Registration of same, fee, etc.—Effects of the passport system—Special passport required to leave Russia—Beneficial results of same 240

CHAPTER XIII

Passenger boats on the Caspian Sea—New lines of steamers—Petrovsk, on the Caspian—Excursion into the mountains—New railway to Baku—Great through line to Central Asia—Important influence of the Trans-Caspian Railway upon the world's affairs—Extension of same into China—Distance and time by this route to China—Direct and short route to Northern India—Projected line of railway from Orenburg to Tashkent—Ambitions of Russia in a new field—Great canal between the Black Sea and the Baltic—Great commercial and strategic importance of same—Steady and persistent progress of Russia—Her advance not rapid, but secure—Does not vaunt her enterprises—Effects upon political world of Trans-Caspian Railway to be greater than the Trans-Siberian Railway—New route from Merv to Herat—Its probable influence on Afghanistan—Projected lines into Persia—Line being built from Armenia to Northern Persia—Important results to arise therefrom in that country—New line projected from Samarkand southward to Karshi—That city the key to Northeastern Afghanistan—Possibility of formidable attack of Russia upon Northern India via Central Asia—No combination of powers could stay it—Unimportant part naval forces would play in such a contest—Russia's contiguous territory and interior operations a manifest advantage—Such a conflict might require the whole power of Great Britain to repel—Russia's peace proposal—Her sin-

cerity in same—Prefers peaceful methods to those of war—
Her superior strategical position—May not Russia's evident
advantage over India operate to preserve peace?—The
fortunate position of America in the event of a great Asiatic
war 261

CHAPTER XIV

The great city of Baku—Its rapid growth—Cause of same—Still
growing rapidly—The petroleum deposits in the Caucasus
—Number of wells in operation—Limited exploration in
Caucasian oil fields—New field north of the Caucasian range
of mountains—Output of the oil wells in 1897—Stories current in Baku—A lucky Tartar—Wonderful wells—Refineries in "Black Town," near Baku—Crude oil extensively
used as fuel in Southern Russia—Desire to visit Central
Asia—Importance of that country politically—The key to
India, Western China, and perhaps Constantinople—Intricacies of European politics—India the real storm-centre—
India indispensable to England's power and greatness—Her
anxiety and efforts to preserve same—Her fear of Russia's
designs upon India—Has relied upon her great navy—Her
naval strength would avail but little to check Russia's advance through Central Asia—Russia's railway building in
Asia regarded as a menace to India—The "gospel of the
machine"—Russian railway advance in Asia—Desire for
alliances—The open door—Cautious measures of Russia in
her Central Asian possessions 281

CHAPTER XV

Admission into Trans-Caspian country—Military railway—Special permit necessary in Trans-Caspian region—Across
Northern Persia—On the Araxes River—First view of Mt.
Ararat—Crossing the Araxes—Mt. Ararat—Grandeur of
same—Ascent of Ararat—Armenian Cemetery—Across the

Araxes Valley—Erivan, the capital of Armenia—Mosques, palaces, etc.—Change under Russian rule—New railway line south of Erivan—Markets in Erivan—The great-tailed sheep—On the road to the Caucasus—Last view of Mt. Ararat—Curious religious sects—Picturesque Lake of Goktcha—Height above the sea—The ancient monastery of Sevanga—Over the Delijan Pass—Descent of northern slope of Armenian mountains—Arrival at Akstafa on the Kura River . 294

CHAPTER XVI

The Caucasus—Its locality and extent—The Kura River—The Rion River—Area of the Caucasus—Population of the same—Mountain ranges—The Greater and Lesser Caucasian Mountains joined by the Suram range—Climate of Caucasia—Products of the soil—Statistics of live stock—Valleys in Eastern Caucasus—Western Caucasia—Roads—Military road from Tiflis to Vladikavkaz—Roads in Southern Caucasia and Armenia—Caucasia the gateway between Europe and Asia—Different races—Tiflis, the capital of Georgia—Its buildings, streets, etc.—The Georgian chieftain, Schemyl—The population of Tiflis—Many military and civil officials—A trip to Borjom, Abbas-Tuman, and Kutais . . 328

CHAPTER XVII

Tiflis to Mtskheta—Great antiquity of that city—Founded by near descendant of Noah—Interesting old bridge—Pompey's conquest of this country—Route over the famous Dariel Pass—Journey up the valley of the Kura River—Soil and climate of the Caucasus—Agricultural operations—Various cereals and other products—Indian corn—Primitive implements—Cattle and buffaloes used to draw the plough—Coöperative operations—Remarkable results in the production of grain in the Caucasus—The cart or arba—The new line of the Trans-Caucasian railway—Petroleum pipe line over Suram Mountains—On the road to Borjom—From Borjom to Abbas-Tuman—Over the Lesser Caucasian Mountains—Soldiers for escorts—Brigands Magnificent view from summit—Kutais—Its history and importance—Rich valley of the Rion—Return to Tiflis . . 349

CHAPTER XVIII

Return to Tiflis—Special permit to visit Central Asia—Great courtesy of the American Ambassador, Hon. E. A. Hitchcock—Return to Baku—Passage across the Caspian Sea—Arrival at Krasnovodsk—A look about that city—Rapid growth of same—Its harbor and other natural advantages—Will become an important city—Railway station—Splendid structure—Curious mixture of natural products—Blending of Oriental and Occidental races—Possible result—Russia's fondness for American products—Use of same in Russia—Her probable future demand for Western products—America's opportunity—Trains on the Trans-Caspian Railway—Courtesy of the railway officials—Emigrants to the far East—Departure from Krasnovodsk—New petroleum field—Minerals and metals here—Uzum-Ada, the old terminus of railway—The plains of Turcomania—Persian Mountains—Central Asia—A vast depressed basin—Caspian Sea below ocean level—Similar depression in Sahara Desert—Russia's Central Asian possessions—Sterility of Turcomania due to lack of rainfall—Oasis of Merv—Strabo's reference to it—Three great level plateaus—Amu-Daria and Syr-Daria Rivers 379

CHAPTER XIX

The old bed of the Amu-Daria River—Across a desert—Oasis of Kizyl-Arvat—Among the Turcomanians—A splendid race—His dwelling—Women in Turcomania—Custom of polygamy—Purchase of wives—Weaving of rugs and carpets—

Their crude device for same—Work done mainly by girls—
Inferiority of the new to the old product—Wealth of the
Turcoman—Their food, clothing, etc.—The camel—Roads
in Turcomania—Caravans of camels—Along the Persian
border — Askabad—New and beautiful city — Vegetable
products of this region—Culture of cotton—Old Teke towns 399

CHAPTER XX

Location of towns on Russian railways—Her occupation of
new countries—Dushak, the southern point of the road—
Irrigation of oasis of Merv—New city of Merv—Railway
from Merv to Herat—Confidence of Russia in Central
Asia—Growth of cotton—The ancient city of Merv—Extraordinary mounds—Home of Kuldja Khan—Curious custom
of naming women—Fertility of the oasis of Merv—Pasture
land and jungles—Wild animals—In the old city of Merv
—Its extent and history—Complete desolation—Home of
wild beasts—Former population—Founded by Alexander
the Great—Its destruction 422

CHAPTER XXI

At Bairom-Ali—Imperial palace—From fertile fields to burning
sands—March of Alexander through the desert—From
sterile sands to fruitful fields—The Amu-Daria River—Its
length, etc.—Quantity of water in the Amu-Daria—Great
railway bridge being erected over the Amu-Daria—Possible diversion of the course of this great river—The slow
and vast operations of nature—Immense deposits of this
great river—Karakul—Rearing of the sheep here known as
Persian lamb 448

CHAPTER XXII

Bokhara—Courtesy of Russian officials—The Ameer of Bokhara—Area and population of Bokhara—Its destruction by
the Tartars—The ruling race—The Usbegs inferior to the

Turcomans—Mosques and colleges—The mosque of Tamerlane in the Reghistan—Inferior to the ruins of Samarkand—Palace of the Ameer of Bokhara—Citadel of Alp-Arslan—Bazaars in Bokhara—Buildings, etc.—Customs, police regulations, etc.—Vices and virtues of the Bokharians—Temperance among the inhabitants—An agreeable contrast—Introduction of opium into Central Asia—An instructive incident 466

CHAPTER XXIII

Bokhara to Samarkand—Residence of Governor of Turkestan—His great civility—Beauty of Samarkand—Avenues of acacias and poplars—The old city of Samarkand—In ruins, but picturesque—Once a great capital—Splendor under the Arabs and under Tamerlane—A seat of learning—Architecture in old city of Samarkand—Colleges in Samarkand—Mosques, tombs, and palaces—The Shah-Zindah—The Tilla-Kari and Khanym—Exquisite effect of tessellated tiles—The great mosque erected by sister of Tamerlane—Similarity of architecture between Central Asia and that of the Moguls in India—A huge pulpit and voluminous Koran . 493

CHAPTER XXIV

Medressehs or colleges in Samarkand—The tomb of Tamerlane—The sarcophagus of the great Tartar—Interior ornamentation—The Russian citadel—Kok-Tash, or throne of Tamerlane—The Shadman-Melik—Its peculiar construction—Excursion in the mountains—The beauty of Samarkand—Reminiscences of Alexander the Great—Social customs, etc.—Polygamy—Peculiar equipage 514

CHAPTER XXV

Natives, or Sarts—Seeing native life and customs—Dinner at the residence of the Amban or native mayor of Samarkand—Our host and his guests—Oriental features of the occasion—Brilliant surroundings—The Russians—The dances—No women as dancers—Boy dancers dressed in the habits of women—The music of the Sart—At first unpleasant—Wherein lies the charm of Oriental music—Due to rhythm—Influence hypnotic—Similar emotional state of howling and dancing dervishes—The dinner—Various native dishes, Kiabab, Cavourna, Pilaf, etc.—Oriental dancing—Producing similar effects by rhythm of motion—Concluding reflections 531

LIST OF ILLUSTRATIONS

Viséed Passport, used by the Author in his Travels in Siberia and Central Asia . . *Frontispiece*	
	PAGE
Trans-Siberian Railway Train—Observation Compartment in Rear Car	7
Railway Officials on Trans-Siberian Railway Train	11
Russian Isvoshtchik, or Droshky Drivers .	14
A Russian Patyorka, or Five-horse Team	15
Group of Peasants in Russian Village	27
Russian Peasant's Log Cabin in Commune or Village . .	29
A Village on the Russian Steppes . . .	30
Syzran on the Volga River .	45
Samara on the Volga River	47
Batraki on the Volga River	49
Great Bridge across the Volga River at Batraki on the Trans-Siberian Railway . . .	51
Russian Village on the Ufa River	53
First View of the Ural Mountains after passing Wajsaowaja, Trans-Siberian Railway	54
The Western Slope of the Ural Mountains on the Trans-Siberian Railway, between Ufa and Zlatoust . . .	55
Station at Zlatoust on Trans-Siberian Railway near the Summit of the Ural Mountains	56
Monument on Summit of Ural Mountains indicating Dividing Line between Europe and Asia . . .	57
Eastern Slope of the Ural Mountains on the Trans-Siberian Railway, Midway between Zlatoust and Tscheljabinsk .	58
Eastern Slope of Ural Mountains on Trans-Siberian Railway, Eighty Miles from the Summit of the Ural Mountains .	59

LIST OF ILLUSTRATIONS

	PAGE
On Trans-Siberian Railway just before arriving at Tscheljabinsk	60
Railway Station at Tscheljabinsk, the End of the First Section of Trans-Siberian Railway, at the Eastern Foot of Ural Mountains	62
Entering the Plains or Steppes of Siberia on the Trans-Siberian Railway, One Hundred Miles East of the Ural Mountains	63
Crossing the Siberian Steppes, Two Hundred Miles East of the Ural Mountains, on the Siberian Railway	64
Kirghiz Tartar Aul or Village on Siberian Steppes	65
View across Siberian Steppes, Three Hundred Miles East of the Ural Mountains	68
Group of Kirghiz Tartars at Station on Siberian Railway	69
On Siberian Steppes, Three Hundred and Fifty Miles East of Ural Mountains	72
On Siberian Steppes, Eight Hundred Miles East of Ural Mountains	72
View across the Irtish River, Siberia	74
Station on Siberian Railway, Four Hundred Miles East of Ural Mountains	75
View across the Ishim River, Siberia	77
On the Tom River, Siberia	78
New Settlement on Open Steppes of Siberia, Six Hundred Miles East of Ural Mountains	79
On Siberian Steppes or Prairies, Four Hundred and Fifty Miles East of the Ural Mountains	81
On Siberian Steppes, between Kurgan and Petropavlovsk	82
Two Views across Siberian Steppes	83
View across Siberian Steppes, Five Hundred Miles East of the Ural Mountains	86
Kirghiz Tartars and Camel Train on Siberian Steppes	88
Railway Bridge over the Obi River on Siberian Railway	89
Railway Station on Siberian Railway, Eight Hundred Miles East of Ural Mountains, or over Two Thousand Miles East of Moscow	91
Station on Siberian Railway	92

LIST OF ILLUSTRATIONS

xxi

PAGE

Sacked Grain awaiting Shipment at the Station on Siberian Railway between Omsk and Tomsk, over One Thousand Miles East of the Ural Mountains 93

Passenger Train for Ordinary Service on Trans-Siberian Railway, making Daily Trips to Tomsk, nearly Three Thousand Miles East of Moscow 94

View on the Siberian Steppes, between the Tobol and Ishim Rivers. Emigrant Train crossing the Steppes to occupy New Lands 95

On the Open Steppes of Siberia, about One Thousand Miles East of the Ural Mountains, or nearly Two Thousand Four Hundred Miles East of Moscow 96

View across Siberian Prairies 97

Distant Herd of Cattle on Siberian Plains or Steppes . . 98

Emigrants at Railway Station between Kainsk and Tomsk on the Trans-Siberian Railway 99

New Settlement on Siberian Railway, One Thousand Miles East of the Ural Mountains 102

View across the Siberian Steppes, Nine Hundred Miles East of the Ural Mountains, or about Two Thousand Two Hundred Miles East of Moscow 104

Recent Settlement on Siberian Railway, One Thousand One Hundred Miles East of Ural Mountains . . . 105

Recent Settlement on Siberian Railway, Nine Hundred and Fifty Miles East of Ural Mountains 107

New Settlement on Siberian Railway, Two Thousand Five Hundred Miles East of Moscow, between Obb and Tomsk 109

New Settlement on Trans-Siberian Railway, One Thousand One Hundred Miles East of the Urals, and between Kriwostchekowo and Kainsk 110

Church in New Town of Obb 111

New Settlement on Siberian Railway, One Thousand Two Hundred and Fifty Miles East of the Urals, or about Two Thousand Five Hundred Miles East of Moscow . . 113

LIST OF ILLUSTRATIONS

	PAGE
Station on the Open Steppes of Siberia on the Trans-Siberian Railway, over One Thousand Miles East of the Ural Mountains, and about Two Thousand Two Hundred Miles East of Moscow	114
On the Siberian Steppes or Prairies, over One Thousand Miles East of the Ural Mountains, and about Two Thousand Two Hundred Miles East of Moscow	115
On the Siberian Steppes, between the Ishim and Irtish Rivers, on the Line of the Siberian Railway	116
Recent Settlement on Siberian Railway, between the Obi and Tom Rivers, about Two Thousand Four Hundred Miles East of Moscow	117
Lake on the Siberian Steppes	118
Emigrants on Siberian Steppes, East of the Obi River	119
Chapel in recently settled Town on Siberian Railway	121
Station at Kurgan, Siberian Railway	124
Kirghiz Tartar, Camels, and Camel Cart	125
Kirghiz Yurt, or Tent, and Group of Tartars on the Siberian Steppes, between Kurgan and Petropavlovsk	127
Tartar Camel Train on Siberian Steppes	129
Church in New Siberian Village	131
A Tartar Dug-out on Road South of Omsk	133
On the Post-route from Petropavlovsk to Omsk	135
Station at Petropavlovsk, Siberian Railway. Group of Kirghiz Tartars	137
Street Scene in Omsk	139
Emigrants at Station, between Petropavlovsk and Omsk, on Siberian Railway	141
Street Scene in Tomsk	143
On the Steppes of Siberia, East of Kurgan	144
Street Scene in Tomsk	145
Distant View of Tomsk	145
Market Scene in Tomsk	147
Village in Siberia, in the Tom River Valley, on the Post-route from Tomsk to Tobolsk	148

LIST OF ILLUSTRATIONS

	PAGE
Emigrant Train between Petropavlovsk and Omsk, Two Thousand Miles East of Moscow	149
View on Post-route, between Tomsk and Irkutsk	151
Patyorka, a Five-horse Team on Siberian Steppes	153
Another Mode of Travelling in Siberia	155
Street Scene in Tomsk	156
Siberian Tarantass	157
Native waiting for Ferry on Tom River	160
Crossing Tom River, Siberia, on a Rude Ferry-boat	161
At the Post-house	163
Taking Tea "Al Fresco" with a Russian Family at Post-house	165
Russian Village on Post-route, South of Tomsk, Siberia	167
Ready to Start. At the Post-house on Post-route, South of Tomsk, in Direction toward Semipalatinsk	168
Cathedral in Tomsk	169
Street Scene in Tomsk	171
Kirghiz Tartar Family on Siberian Steppes. The Tartar Yurt or Tent	173
Great Forty-ton Bell at Cathedral in Tomsk	177
On the Turf at Tomsk	179
On the Home Stretch	181
Street Scene in Tomsk	183
Washerwomen at Tomsk	185
Railway Station on Siberian Railway, between the Obi and Tom Rivers, about One Thousand One Hundred Miles East of the Ural Mountains	187
Station on the Trans-Siberian Railway, between Tomsk and Tiaga	189
Street Scene in Astrakhan	193
On the Volga River	195
Fire Worshippers' Temple in Astrakhan	196
The Kremlin in Astrakhan	197
Scene on the Landing at Astrakhan	199
View of the Upper Town of Nijni Novgorod, on North Bank of the Volga	201

LIST OF ILLUSTRATIONS

	PAGE
Town on the Volga River, between Kazan and Nijni Novgorod	204
View of Nijni Novgorod, where the Great Fair is held, on South Side of the Volga	205
Picturesque Formation on the Volga River, Two Hundred Miles above Astrakhan	208
The Cathedral in Nijni Novgorod	209
Watermelon Market at Landing on the Volga River, between Simbirsk and Saratov	211
Fishing Village on the Obi River, Siberia	213
Town on the Lower Volga River	215
View across Tom River, Siberia	216
Ferry-boat on Tom River, Siberia	218
Houses for Storage of Grain and Wheat in Sacks awaiting Shipment at New Railway Station, Eight Hundred Miles East of the Ural Mountains, on Trans-Siberian Railway	219
Scene on the Irtish River, Siberia	220
View across the Irtish River, Siberia	221
View across the Tom River, Siberia	222
Wharf-boat and Landing on Volga River, below Tzaritzin	225
Town on the Volga River	238
Village in Siberia, between Tomsk and the Yenisei River	241
Houses in Small Siberian Town, on the Post-road to Tobolsk	243
Dwelling-house in Siberian Village, on Post-route from Tiaga to Tomsk	245
Siberian Village in Obi Valley	246
New Village in the Valley of the Tom River, Siberia	247
Cask of Water at Station on Siberian Railway, supplied with Boiled Water for Use of Passengers	251
The Great Petroleum City of Baku, on the Caspian Sea, in the Eastern Caucasus. View from the Bay	262
General View of the City of Baku	263
Cathedral in Baku	266
Railway Station in Baku	269
General View of the City and Harbor of Baku	280
Oil Field South of Baku, near the Shore of the Caspian Sea, operated by English and French Capitalists	282

LIST OF ILLUSTRATIONS

	PAGE
Oil Field Northwest of Baku, Several Hundred Feet above the Sea Level, operated by Swedish and French Capitalists	284
A Celebrated Spouter	287
Interior of the Ancient Palace of the Viceroys of Persia in Erivan	295
Caravan crossing the Araxes River, on the Borders of Russia and Persia, en route for Erivan, Armenia	297
On the Banks of the Araxes River, forming the Boundary between Russia and Persia	298
Group of Natives at Kamerlu	299
In the Valley of the Araxes River. Little and Great Ararat Mountains in the Distance	301
Distant View of Mt. Ararat	302
Rude Ferry across the Araxes River	303
On the Road to Mt. Ararat	307
Cossack Cavalrymen on the Road to Mt. Ararat	309
Returning from Mt. Ararat	310
Persian Cart or Arba	311
Market Scene in Erivan. Great Fat-tailed Sheep	312
An Armenian Cemetery	313
View of Mt. Ararat, looking Southward from Erivan, the Capital of Armenia	315
New Mosque of Huessin Ali Khan in Erivan	316
Street Scene in Erivan	317
Ancient Mohammedan Mosque in Erivan	319
A Dukobortsi Village—a Religious Sect in Northern Armenia —on the Road from Erivan to Tiflis	320
Regiment of Cossacks on their Way to Northern Border of Persia, on the Araxes River	321
Threshing Grain in Armenia	324
Little Island in Lake Goktcha, on which the Ancient Monastery of Sevanga is located	324
Skoptsy Village—a Peculiar Religious Sect with Remarkable Customs—in Northern Armenia	325
On the Road to Lake Sevanga, in Northern Armenia, and on the Route from Elnofka to Akstafa	326

LIST OF ILLUSTRATIONS

	PAGE
On the Northern Slope of the Lesser Caucasian Mountains, after leaving the Delijan Pass	327
General View of the City of Tiflis	329
Street Scene in Tiflis	332
View of Tiflis from the Fortress above the City	333
Street Scene in Tiflis	335
Valley of the Kura River, about One Hundred Miles East of Tiflis, and in the Vicinity of Akstafa	336
Floating Water-mills on the Kura River in the City of Tiflis	337
Caucasians and Their Costumes	340
Funeral Cortége in Tiflis	341
The Theatre in Tiflis	343
Mounted Cossacks in Public Square in the City of Tiflis	344
A Bazaar in the Persian Quarter in the City of Tiflis	345
Street Scene in the Persian Quarter in Tiflis	346
Street Scene in the Persian Quarter of Tiflis	347
General View of Tiflis, from Elevation in Western Part of the City, looking Eastward	350
On the Kura River, in the Western Suburbs of Tiflis, on the Road to Borjom	351
In the Kura Valley, between Tiflis and Mtskheta	352
On the Kura River, Caucasia, near Mtskheta	353
In the Valley of the Aragva, on the Military Road over the Caucasian Mountains, from Tiflis to Vladikavkaz	355
Over the Dariel Pass, on Military Road from Tiflis to Vladikavkaz. Mount Kasbek in the Distance	356
Ploughing in the Kura Valley	357
Scene in a Farm Village on the Aragva	360
Scene between Mikhailov and Borjom	361
Cart, or Arba, used for Farm and Road Purposes	363
View near Gori, on the Kura River	365
In the Kura Valley	367
Persian Minister's Residence in Borjom	368
The Summer Palace of His Imperial Highness the Grand Duke Michael, on the Banks of the Kura River, near Borjom	369

LIST OF ILLUSTRATIONS xxvii

	PAGE
His Imperial Highness Grand Duke Michael on his Daily Drive in Borjom	370
Market Scene in Kutais	371
Soldier on the Mountain Side, after leaving Abbas-Tuman, on the Road to Kutais, over the Lesser Caucasian Mountains	373
Street Scene in Kutais	374
On the Summit of the Lesser Caucasian Mountains. Russian and Cossack Guards	375
Market Scene in Kutais	377
Krasnovodsk and Harbor, the Western Terminus of the Trans-Caspian Railway, on the Eastern Shore of the Caspian Sea	382
New Railway Station at Krasnovodsk, the Western Terminus of the Trans-Caspian Railway	384
Trans-Caspian Railway Train	387
New Oil Wells recently opened on the Shores of the Caspian Sea, on the Line of Railway below Krasnovodsk	390
Russian Military Encampment on Open Plains	391
Station on Trans-Caspian Railway	394
View across the Plains of Turcomania, between Askabad and Dushak, on the Trans-Caspian Railway	396
Turcomanian Tartars at Kizyl-Arvat, Station on the Trans-Caspian Railway	400
Turcomanians and their Yurts or Tents	401
Turcoman Village on the Plains of Turcomania, between Kizyl-Arvat and Askabad	403
Turcoman Tents	405
Turcoman Tartars at Geok-Tepe, Station on the Trans-Caspian Railway	406
Turcoman Girls weaving Carpets under a Temporary Canopy adjoining their Tent	408
Turcoman Tent on the Plains of Tartary	409
Camel Caravan crossing the Plains of Turcomania	411
View across the Desert of Turcomania, looking toward the Persian Mountains	414
Turcoman Village on the Open Plains, between Geok-Tepe and Askabad	415

LIST OF ILLUSTRATIONS

	PAGE
Station at Askabad, on Trans-Caspian Railway	416
Station of Dju-dju-kly, on the Trans-Caspian Railway	417
Scene near Askabad	418
Irrigating Canals in Oasis of Merv	419
Extraordinary Mounds near Merv	423
Home of Kuldja Khan	426
Distant View of Old City of Merv	427
Gateway into Old City of Merv	429
In the Old City of Merv	433
In the Old City of Merv	435
Walls and Gateway of the Old City of Merv	437
Distant View of Merv	439
Ruined Mosque of the Sultan Sanjare	440
Ruined Mosque in Old City of Merv	441
Old Walls around Ancient City of Merv	444
Old Wall and Gateway in City of Merv	445
Across the Desert	449
Station at Bairom-Ali on Trans-Caspian Railway, on the Road to Bokhara	451
Bundles of Fagots used as a Sand Barrier to protect the Railway against the Drifting Sand	452
Market Scene in the Town of Amu-Daria, on the Banks of the Amu-Daria River	453
On the Amu-Daria, above the City of that Name	455
Temporary Railway Bridge over the Amu-Daria River	457
Street in Amu-Daria	459
Railway Station at the New, or Russian, Town of Bokhara, the Old City being Twelve Miles from the Railway	460
New Palace being built by Russia for the Ameer of Bokhara, near the Station in the New, or Russian, Town of that Name	462
Old Mosque said to have been built by Tamerlane	463
Summer Palace of the Ameer of Bokhara, between the New and Old Cities of that Name	464
The Ameer of Bokhara	467

LIST OF ILLUSTRATIONS

xxix

PAGE

Tower formerly used to execute Criminals by throwing them from the Top 469
Reghistan, or Market-place, in Bokhara, near the Old Citadel . 471
Old Mosque, covered with Variegated Tiles 472
Bazaar in Bokhara 473
A Graveyard in the City of Bokhara 475
Native Bokharians, Father and Sons 477
The Citadel in Bokhara, said to have been built by Alp-Arslan, the Persian King 479
Muezzin calling the Faithful to Prayer from the Minaret of a Mosque in Bokhara 480
View over the Roofs of the Houses in Bokhara . . 481
Bazaar in Bokhara 483
Street and Old Mosque in the Neighborhood of the Reghistan, or Market-place 484
Ruined Minaret, encased with Beautiful Variegated Tiles . 485
Ruins of Ancient Mosque near the Reghistan, in Bokhara . 487
Irrigating Canals on the Plains of Bokhara, on the Road to Samarkand. Water drawn from the Zerafshan River . 488
Palace of the Ameer of Bokhara . . . 489
College, or Medresseh, in Bokhara 492
Park in the City of Samarkand, in Front of the Tomb of Tamerlane 494
Street Scene in Samarkand 495
Mosque near the Reghistan, built by Tamerlane, in Samarkand 497
Mosque near Centre of City, built by Tamerlane, called the Tilla-Kari 498
Street Scene in Samarkand 499
Street Scene in Samarkand, showing the Mosque of Khanym, erected by Tamerlane to his Favorite Wife, a Chinese Princess 501
Street Scene in Samarkand 502
Mohammedans at Prayer 503
Entrance to the Mosque Shah-Zindah. Tessellated Tiles, with Variegated Coloring 505
Medresseh, or Native College, in Old Samarkand . 507

LIST OF ILLUSTRATIONS

	PAGE
Street Scene in Samarkand. Street leading from Railway Station to the Citadel in the City	509
Ruins of the Mosque built by Sister of Tamerlane	510
Great Marble Pulpit in Front of Mosque built by Tamerlane's Sister	511
Interior of Tamerlane's Tomb. His Sarcophagus and those of his Son and Prime Minister	515
Street Scene in the New, or Russian, City of Samarkand	517
Tomb of Tamerlane, located on the Edge of a Great Park in the New, or Russian, City of Samarkand	518
Kok-Tash, or Throne of Tamerlane	519
Entrance to the Tomb of Tamerlane	521
Exterior of Tomb of Tamerlane, in New, or Russian, City of Samarkand	522
The Shadman-Malik, or Bridge of Tamerlane	523
Street Scene in Samarkand	525
Burial Place of Mohammedan Saints, near the Great Mosque of the Tilla-Kari, in Samarkand	526
A Queer Equipage. A Mohammedan and his Wives out for a Drive	527
Market Scene in Samarkand	529
A Mohammedan and his Wives. Scene in the Park in the New, or Russian, City of Samarkand	532
Natives, or Sarts. Father and Son	533
Medresseh, or Native College, located in the Old City of Samarkand	534
Street Scene in the Old City of Samarkand, leading from the Public Square to the Great Mosque of Tamerlane	535
In the Old City of Samarkand, Street leading to the Great Mosque of the Shah-Zindah. Native Sarts in the Foreground	536
Street Scene in the Russian, or New, City of Samarkand	537
Ruins of the Mosque of the Shah-Zindah, in the Old City of Samarkand	538
Entrance through the Enclosing Wall that surrounds the Tomb of Tamerlane, in the City of Samarkand	539

LIST OF ILLUSTRATIONS xxxi

	PAGE
View in the Park in the Old City of Samarkand	540
Dancers and Musicians at Banquet in Samarkand	541
Native Musicians in the Old City of Samarkand	543
Dancers at Banquet in the Old City of Samarkand	544
Shadman-Malik, or Bridge of Tamerlane, over the Zerafshan River, Twenty Miles from City of Samarkand	545
Market Scene in the Old City of Samarkand	546
Street Scene in the New Town of Samarkand	547

SIBERIA AND CENTRAL ASIA

I

Trans-Siberian railway—Its commercial and political importance—The effect it has already produced—Russia's military strength—Napoleon's estimate of Russian soldiers—Probable international complications to arise from Russia's industrial advance eastward—Our own relation thereto—General features of the Trans-Siberian railway—The trains and their equipment—Travel on the post-routes of Russia—Humane law respecting horses.

Moscow, *July*, 1898.

I AM starting, in a few hours, on a long and somewhat trying journey right into the depths of Siberia. As most of my trip will be done on the new Trans-Siberian railway, you may be perhaps interested in the facts and details I have thus far been enabled to collect concerning this extraordinary enterprise, destined, as I believe, to have more far-reaching political, commercial, and even ethnological influences than any industrial and economic scheme that has ever been conceived or executed.

It constitutes the first link in the great chain that will bind in close union, harmony, and sympathy, two of the mightiest branches of the human family, having racial and traditional affinities, and embracing almost one-half of the human race.

Even in its partially completed condition, it has already perceptibly tilted the political and commercial world on its axis. It has thrown England into a state of great alarm for the safety of India, and has caused that descent of other European nations upon the China littoral, where, in a limited area, there is to be much future strife, wrangling, and, perhaps, profitless warfare.

It almost takes one's breath away to contemplate the tremendous consequences that must ensue when, through material or other agencies, peoples whose wondrous past and present achievements suggest vast latent possibilities, are united by a common interest and policy. One can almost see the certain absorption of Persia and the Ottoman Empire on the one hand, and India on the other. In such an event, the world may see four-fifths of its population acting in accord, the permanence of which is guaranteed by ethnical affinities.

In this view it must not be forgotten that, on account of the impenetrability of this vast region, no combination of forces could prevent or even arrest the execution of policies and schemes that diplomacy or interest might suggest. The history of Russia alone points a valuable lesson in this connection. Of her population nearly nine-tenths are engaged in agriculture. It is not in this respect alone that she retains the characteristics of her ancient pastoral progenitors. The retreat of the Scythians before the hosts of Darius, described by Herodotus with such lively interest, until the invincible armies of Persia were worn out by the pursuit of a foe that would not fight and could not be captured; the destruction of the legions under Crassus, which gave rise to the Roman proverb, "The retreat of the Parthians was more to be dreaded than the advance of any other army;" down to the burning of Moscow by Rostopchin, which resulted in the annihilation of the greatest army and the greatest captain the world ever saw; shows that, like her ancestors, she possesses and is ready to use the most fatal of resources.

But the military strength of Russia lies not alone in this negative resource—which will ultimately prove true of all Asiatic races—as she surpasses all other nations in the extent of her armament. Her standing army is computed at 1,500,000 to 2,000,000 of men, and she could quickly put herself on a war footing of four or five millions of men well appointed and equipped. In St. Petersburg alone there are no less than 100,000, in Moscow 150,000, in the Crimea 150,000, in Poland 160,000, and it is said that there are also a quarter of a million in the Caucasus alone, and it is more than hinted that a large army is even now quartered in Tibriz, the second city in Persia.

As by act of 1873 all able-bodied subjects of the empire have to give a certain number of years of active service in the army, one can form some idea of what a vast military element exists among 130,000,000 of people, and which could, under an emergency, be quickly materialized into an available army.

They are, moreover, of the best fighting material in the world, being obedient, patient, subservient to rule and discipline, and rugged and hardy, unequalled, perhaps, by any other race.

When looking at the splendid armies one sees everywhere, one does not wonder at Napoleon's saying after his reverse at Moscow, "that if he had an army of Russians, it would not be long before the universe had but one god and the world only one emperor." The discomfiture of the English at Pekin at the hands of Pavloff, and the still more recent and equally humiliating one at the court of Persia by the Russian minister there, shows that Russia is as skilful and powerful in diplomacy as in the field. Her recent appropriation of 90 millions of dollars—making over 300 millions within a few years—for the building of iron-clads, caused

England to hastily revise her budget, attended with ugly rumors of the necessity of some sort of conscription.

The spectre of approaching Russian Asiatic domination, with its sure bearing upon India, no doubt has led to the recent frantic desire of England for alliances, even when of the most incongruous nature. Our own country has a destiny apart from all other nations, and I hope it will keep clear of all those complications that would hamper it in its right growth and development. No nation has ever equalled the Americans in those admirable qualities so necessary for the settlement and development of new countries.

This is our special province and our appointed destiny, and in the Western Hemisphere alone there will be for all time an ample field wherein to exercise our choicest energies and abilities. If we prove true to ourselves and our manifest duties, and allow no dissipation of our energies and forces by becoming involved in the intricate affairs of remote countries, but confine our expansive forces to the Western Hemisphere, we will quickly build up an empire second to none. I should regret to see our country lose its "free hand" by any alliance which in these days of growing international complications must prove entangling. It would be especially undesirable with a nation under whose gentle allurements of philanthropy and "unrestricted trade," and much display of "unctuous rectitude," there too often lies the covert desire to use other people in the accomplishment of her selfish aims.

Excuse this digression. I set out to simply write you of my Siberian trip. The line of the Trans-Siberian railway runs in a general way through middle European Russia, the centre of the southern part of Western Siberia, and along the southern border of Eastern Siberia. Its western terminus is Moscow, and in the east, Vladivostok on the Pacific Ocean. It is difficult to determine its exact length, as the recent Russian-Chinese relations that have sprung up have caused Russia to change the original route down the Amur River in East Siberia. A commission has recently left here to make a new survey from a point about 1,200 miles west of Vladivostok, with the intention of radiating from that point several lines through Manchuria eastward, as China has recently given Russia extensive concessions in that province. One of these lines will run direct to Vladivostok through Manchuria, and, joining with the main line from Moscow, will thus make a much shorter route than the one originally designed to run down the Amur River, of which nearly 1,000 miles is now completed. Even under the new survey the line will not be less than 6,100 miles long.

There is now completed about 4,000 miles of road from Moscow east, on which trains are run-

TRANS-SIBERIAN RAILWAY TRAIN.—OBSERVATION COMPARTMENT IN REAR CAR

ning. On the last 1,000 miles, however, only construction trains are running, with an occasional mixed passenger train at intervals of about a fortnight. In the last six weeks they have put on a through train that runs from Moscow to Tomsk, on the Tom River. This train leaves once in ten days and furnishes fairly comfortable facilities. Ordinary trains that break the journey at many points run also, at irregular intervals, as far as Omsk. The distance from Moscow to Tomsk is about 3,000 miles. It is the through train that I am taking. Whatever expeditions I make east of Tomsk will have to be done on construction trains, or over the old Siberian post-route by troikas or droshkies—curious vehicles drawn by three or five horses.

It is most difficult to get anything like accurate information concerning either this great line or the country along the road east of the Volga River, as few travellers as yet have gone into that region. Judging, however, from what I see here at the western terminus of the road, everything is being done in the most thorough manner, and indicates that the Russian is fully alive to the great value this road will be to the Empire, and the marvellous changes to be wrought by it.

The station here, at which the line begins, is a marvel of architecture. Next to that of the Grand India Peninsular Railroad in Bombay, it is the most splendid railway station I have ever seen. In its features, it furnishes additional evidence of what

you discover on all hands as you go eastward, of
the fusion of things Occidental and Oriental. In
this structure the bizarre effect produced by the
blending of the plain, practical materiality of the
West with the florid idealism of the East is at
once surprising and charming. It is more like a
palace than a railway station.

The Government (for almost all railways here
are run by the Government) is most active in its
preparations for the future operation of the road.
I was shown a train in course of preparation that
is to be one of the many that are to run over the
entire length of the line when completed. The
scale of magnificence upon which they are to be
operated is a surprise even to one familiar with
the splendor of our own metropolitan trains.

The trains will be composed wholly of sleep-
ing, parlor, and dining cars, an elegant salon occupying fully one-half of each car at the middle,
having piano, writing-tables, maps, library, etc.
Besides the usual toilet-room there is an elegant
bath-room, where at a small cost we can have a
warm or cold bath. There is also to be a room
fitted up especially for gymnastic exercise, with
dumb-bells, frictional apparatus for muscular development, and all the newest belongings of such
an establishment. The trains will be of the ves-
tibule type, with electric lights and signals, air

brakes, and other first-class accessories. In addition to the general director of the train, each car has for its service a porter and a special guard, so that a train of seven or eight passenger coaches will have from twenty to thirty officials and employees connected with it. In fine, when once in full operation, they will, in luxury and comfort, more resemble a trans-Atlantic steamship than a trans-Asiatic railway train.

The compartments, on account of extreme height and size, will have an airy comfort quite in agreeable contrast with the low ceilings and stuffy character of many of our first-class cars. Not least of the inspiring things of this great enterprise is the low fare that will be charged, being less than one cent and a half per mile, including expense of sleeping-car. As the through trains can be run at thirty to thirty-four miles per hour, the trip from Moscow to Vladivostok will ultimately be made in eight to nine days. It is not among the improbable things that within ten years one can make a continuous trip from Paris to Pekin, a distance of something over 8,000 miles.

If this route does not become the most interesting and agreeable in the world, it will not be the fault of the Russian government. One can form some feeble notion of the vast future possibilities

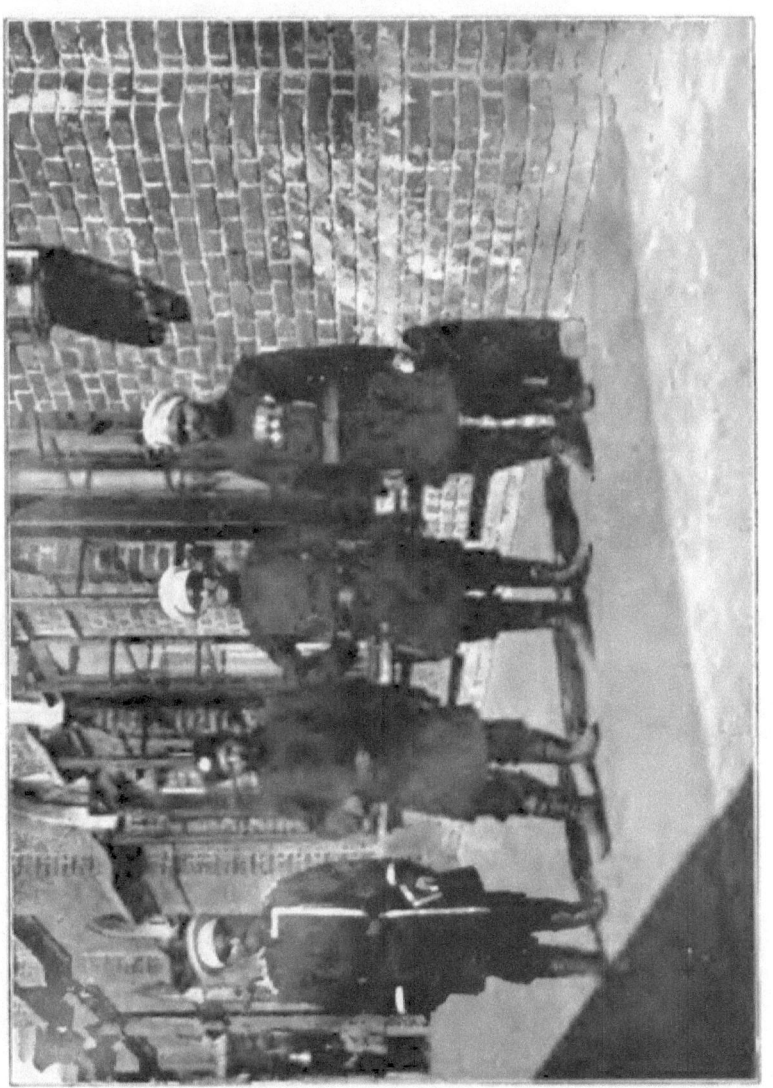

RAILWAY OFFICIALS ON TRANS-SIBERIAN RAILWAY TRAIN

when we reflect that it is the connecting link between 500 millions of people in the east and 300 millions in the west. It is my intention to go to Irkutsk, and also to Tobolsk, if the journey by the old post-route does not prove too fatiguing. Post travel is anything but a luxury in Russia. Although the roads on the main routes are excellent, almost equal to those in France, the troikas are much wanting in comfort, and the Isvoshtchik is a furious driver and the horses are spirited.

They usually have from three to five horses, according to condition of road, and hitched abreast. The posts are about eighteen versts—twelve miles—apart, where relays are secured. When ready to start, the driver takes the lines in his hands, and scarcely touches his seat when the horses suddenly spring into a full gallop, which pace they keep right up until the next post is reached. A distance of 200 miles can thus readily be covered in a day; that is, in a day and night. The driver, however, is a lazy fellow, and a vast amount of time is needlessly wasted in the change of horses. Were it not for this delay, 250 miles or more might easily be made. I am told that in some cases military and other officials make over 300 miles in a day on sledges in the winter.

Speaking of horses, there is a notable law in effect in most of the large Russian towns concerning them, that deserves especial mention. Among the curious things that arrest the attention on arriving in Moscow, is the entire absence of whips

RUSSIAN ISVOSHTCHIK, OR DROSHKY DRIVERS

among the drivers of carriages, cabs, and all sorts of vehicles. On inquiry, I was informed that there was a law prohibiting their use or in any way punishing a horse. I don't believe there is a single whip in use in Moscow. Even to strike a horse with a catch of the lines is forbidden, and punished

A RUSSIAN PAITORKA, OR FIVE-HORSE TEAM

if discovered. The excellent condition of the horses fully attests the benefits of this humane law. Nothing can exceed the beauty of the sleek and well-groomed horses used in the carriages of Moscow.

I have succeeded in securing the services of an excellent valet. He is a Caucasian, a native of Tiflis. His native language is Russian, but he speaks English quite well, as also French, German, Italian, Swedish, Tartar, and almost everything else. Although he has never been to Siberia, still his knowledge of the country and its customs will render him most useful to me. I will write you again when I get beyond the Volga River and Ural Mountains, where the novel attractions of Asiatic Russia really begin.

II

The Russian steppes—Their similarity to the prairies and plains of the United States—The lands of Russia—Geological division of the same—The great Tschernoziom lands of Russia—Their capacity and products—System of farming in Russia—The yearly production of cereals—Exports of same—Russian live stock and emport statistics—Manufacturing and mining industries—Culture of Indian corn—Population of Russia—Distribution of same—The rural and urban population of Russia—Dwellings and other buildings in the villages.

Tscheljabinsk, Siberia, *August*, 1889.

I am writing you from Tscheljabinsk (pronounced Chee-lay-ah-binsk), a small but interesting and picturesque town 100 miles east of the Ural Mountains, and about 1,400 miles east of Moscow. The route I have come, therefore, is much the same as going from Indianapolis to Denver.

Not only in distance does the comparison hold, but in a striking manner in a geographic and physical sense also. To all Americans who have travelled to the Rocky Mountains through the States of Illinois, Minnesota, Iowa, Kansas, and Nebraska, the country I have come through is easy to describe. To simply say it is exactly like it would constitute a more or less perfect description. Indeed, I have never seen any two things more absolutely similar than are the prairie and plain regions of our country and that vast region lying in southeast Russia, extending from Tula east to the Ural Mountains, a distance of over 1,000 miles, and from Nijni Novgorod south to the Caspian Sea, a distance of 1,200 miles. It is called by the Russians Tschernoziom, or black earth. It is also known as the steppe, which is Russian for prairie. The soil is black, and seems identical with that of Illinois and Iowa, although, I think, somewhat stronger than in those States.

To generalize crudely, the lands of Russia would be divided into two classes: the woodland, covering the northern part and composed of the rougher elements or detritus of the ancient glacier that once spread over the greater part of Russia, and by whose action its varied soils were produced; and the Tschernoziom, covering in a general way the southern half of the country.

The first is covered mainly with forests, marshes, and sand wastes, although interspersed with many deposits of vegetable mould, giving more or less important areas for culture. The Tschernoziom region is almost coincident with that of the steppe. It extends in a northeastern direction over thirty or forty of the largest provinces of Russia, from

Podolia and Bessarabia in the southwest, to Ufa and the Urals in the east, and from the Black Sea to Moscow.

This formation is of surpassing fertility, and within its limits the greater portion of the nation's agricultural surplus is produced. It covers an area of something like 300 millions of acres, and in its productive capacity must exceed that of the other lands in European Russia.

Spring wheat, rye, oats—indeed, all the cereals grow here in the most wonderful manner in a fair season, and every acre is under a good state of cultivation.

The system of farming practised throughout the Tschernoziom region and much in vogue in the steppe formations generally, such as the Kuban and Don Cossack regions in southern Volga districts and the northern Caucasus, is what is known as the resting system. It is simply the alternation of cereal crops at stated intervals with pasturage. By giving up the lands to pasture that have been cropped for several years with various grains, the soil recuperates naturally without much aid of artificial fertilizers. It is practically the same method followed by many of our own farmers, and known as converting cultivated fields into fallow lands.

There will therefore be found, throughout great areas, many open fields devoted to grazing, and supporting great herds of cattle, sheep, horses, and other domestic animals, interspersed among fields devoted to the culture of rye, wheat, oats, spelt, and other cereals.

A few statistics as to what Russia is producing in the way of grains, while they may not prove interesting, may at least be instructive. In 1893-94, in the fifty governments of European Russia—not including Finland and Poland—there was a little over 24,000,000 of desetines, or about 65,000,000 acres, given to rye, which in this country ranks as of first importance, and constitutes the main article of food consumed by the masses, especially the peasantry. This will serve to explain why so large a proportion of a relatively small wheat crop is exported to foreign markets.

Just here it may be well to take some note of Russia's grain shipments to foreign countries. During the six years from 1888 to 1893 inclusive, which also embraces the famine year of 1890-91, her exports of all grains amounted to an annual average of 380,000,000 pouds, or nearly 220,000,000 bushels. Of this total, 320,000,000 pouds, or a little over 200,000,000 bushels, was made up of the four great cereal staples—wheat, rye, barley, and oats; wheat alone accounts for an annual average during those years of 150,000,000 pouds, or 90,000,000 bushels; oats, 58,000,000 bushels;

barley, 40,000,000 bushels, and rye, 41,000,000 bushels. Thus it will be seen that, estimating by weight, wheat constituted during those years almost half of the gross grain exports. The total value of Russia's entire annual exports and imports is about $700,000,000, and the value of her exports exceeds that of her imports by about $150,000,000 per annum.

The outturn of rye for 1893-94 was nearly 700,000,000 bushels. Of the lands given to this crop, I might add that nearly 19,000,000 desetines, or about three-fourths, belong to the peasants, and the remaining 5,000,000 to the large landed proprietors. Both spring and winter wheats are cultivated, the latter mainly in the southern and southeastern governments, and the former in the western portion and the higher latitudes. They are, moreover, produced in the proportion of about six acres of the former to three of the latter.

In 1893-94 there were 240,000,000 bushels of wheat produced, of which the peasants are accredited with the usual proportion of six-tenths. Oats were cultivated to the extent of 36,000,000 acres, with a yield of nearly 600,000,000 bushels. The yield of barley was 136,000,000 bushels, and of buckwheat 60,000,000 bushels. Besides, some 40,000,000 acres were devoted to other cereals, such as millet, pease, spelt, potatoes, etc.

It might also be mentioned as an important feature in the agriculture of this country that the beet-sugar industry is a large and rapidly growing one. In 1893 there were 800,000 acres under beets, yielding 35,000,000 pounds, or about 600,000 tons of sugar. To manufacture this there were, at that time, 230 factories in Russia, employing some 90,000 persons.

There were in Russia in 1893, 26,000,000 horses, over 34,000,000 cattle, 65,000,000 sheep, and over 12,000,000 swine. The dairy interest is large, widely diffused, and rapidly growing. Beside, supplying almost incalculable quantities for home consumption, butter, cheese, and other products of this industry are extensively exported. From 1886 to 1893 the annual average exportation was, of cheese nearly 3,000,000 pounds, and of butter 16,000,000 pounds.

Live stock is an important article of export, and of wool there is an annual exportation of 70,000,000 pounds. It may not be an uninteresting fact to mention that of the rather insignificant item of hogs' bristles over 6,000,000 pounds are sent to foreign countries yearly.

Having given somewhat in detail the agricultural capabilities and products of Russia, it may be well to here present briefly, in so far as available statistics may disclose, what she is doing in the way of manufacturing. In 1892, there were in Russia 34,680 manufactories, employing nearly 1,500,000 operatives and workmen, producing about $800,000,000 worth of products, or an annual output of $550 for each workman.

Of this number there were 2,350 manufactories engaged in producing cotton, linen, woollen, and kindred fabrics, and employing 425,200 operatives. Nearly 3,000 factories were engaged in making leather goods. Of flour, starch, malt, wool, sawmills, and others of like nature, there were 8,150, employing 80,000 operatives. Of cast-iron there were produced in 1890 about 1,200,000 tons, employing 233,000 workmen. There were 1,881 manufactories and mills engaged in producing iron, steel, machinery, and other metal products, employing 118,000 workmen, with an annual turnover of about $100,000,000. In nearly 2,000 mines (gold, copper, platinum, silver, lead, tin, and other metals), there were employed 106,000 workmen.

The flax and hemp products of Russia merit especial mention, since it easily ranks the rest of the world in this important industry. In 1890-91 the entire world's crop of flax fibre was 1,102,-600,000 pounds. Of this total Russia produced 630,000,000 of pounds, or nearly sixty per cent. In that year Russia produced 306,400,000 pounds

PRODUCTION OF FLAX AND HEMP

of hemp fibre, or near forty per cent. of the entire European crop.

It will thus be seen that of these two valuable staples Russia is to be credited with nearly one-half of the world's product. Of this amount she gathers yearly, about one-third is consumed in her own mills, and in this branch of manufacturing she stands second only to Great Britain, having in operation 420,000 spindles and 13,000 looms, or more than one-third of those in operation in the United Kingdom, and somewhat in excess of either France, Germany, Italy, or other European states. Her exports of flax and hemp fibre are over 500,000,000 pounds annually.

Without a moment's intermission, you see on all hands the landscape stretching away in interminable prairies and rolling plains. As in our own country, it is traversed by a few large rivers and many small streams, and by those peculiar western gullies or draws, fringed with shrubbery.

On looking out of the car window, were it not for the quaint appearance of the people, with their queer, particolored costumes, the Saracenic aspect imparted by the mosque-like churches, with their rich coloring and gilded domes, that dot the landscape everywhere, one would think he was in Illinois or Nebraska. The land, like our western plains, supports a rich herbage, and is covered with great herds of cattle, sheep, horses, etc. While the cattle are neither so large nor well bred as in America, still they furnish an excellent beef; in fact, I never ate a finer beefsteak than you will get along the route at the hotels and railway restaurants.

To an American, the one great difference between this and the great West is the conspicuous absence of Indian corn. As this is about latitude fifty-six degrees, being nearly 1,000 miles north of the Ohio River, it will not mature here, but in South Russia and the Caucasus it grows and matures quite as well as in America.

The area of Indian corn in Russia proper is given at only a little over 1,000,000 acres, with a production of 18,000,000 bushels. This is, however, confined to a small extent of country closely bordering on the Black Sea. In the northern Caucasus, however, and the western part of the trans-Caucasian region, immense quantities are grown, and yield a large surplus for foreign markets.

The distribution of population in Russia is somewhat peculiar. As I have before said, nearly nine-tenths of the people are engaged in agriculture, and only from ten per cent. to fourteen per cent. live in the cities.

In 1893, out of a total population in European

GROUP OF PEASANTS IN RUSSIAN VILLAGE

Russia of 91,800,000, including the governments of Finland and Poland, about 80,000,000 were residents of the country and only 12,000,000 lived in the cities. In Asiatic Russia (Siberia, the Cau-

RUSSIAN PEASANT'S LOG CABIN IN COMMUNE OR VILLAGE

casus, and Central Asia), even a more marked disproportion exists, as out of a total population of 18,000,000 in those countries, less than 2,000,000 were dwellers in the cities.

There are a few grand cities like St. Petersburg, Moscow, Warsaw, and Odessa, with from 250,000 to over 1,000,000 inhabitants; then there are quite a number of cities of 40,000 to 150,000 inhab-

A VILLAGE ON THE RUSSIAN STEPPES

itants; after that, there are none that possess the features of a great city, or that can be classed as such. The rest of the population is wholly contained in farm villages or communes of from 50 to 300 or 400 families (as the Russian farmer rarely lives on his farm), scattered in immense numbers throughout the country. It is not an uncommon thing that a dozen of these villages are in sight at one time.

The buildings of these villages are mostly of wood and thatched. Many of them are made of of logs and much resemble the primitive log cabin the West. Being, however, more ornate in exterior finish, and in contour resembling very much the Swiss chalet, they often have a pleasing effect. There invariably rises out of the midst of these villages an imposing church edifice, always of the Greek Church, most beautiful in its exquisite proportions and rich coloring.

III

Emancipation of the serfs—Peasants now great land-owners—Emancipation rescript of Alexander II., in 1861—Condition of the serfs prior to this act—General provisions of emancipation rescript—Obligatory redemption of lands—Measures to facilitate same—Distribution and allotment of lands to the serfs—Division of serfs into three categories—Effects of emancipation act—Its tendency to lessen conflict between capital and labor—Devotion of the peasant to his lot acquired by this act—An impediment to emigration to Siberia and other distant lands—Russia's position in the probable clash of nations—Number of serfs liberated under the emancipation act—Date of the proclamation—The peaceful accomplishment of this great act—Peace rescript of the present Czar—Is Russia rightly understood by other nations?

IN no country, perhaps, not even excepting France, where the desire to possess land assumes almost the form of a mania, is there to be found a class so supremely a land-owning class as the peasantry of Russia. Excluding a few provinces in Finland, Poland, and the Baltic, it is rare to find among the peasants of this country one who does not possess a lot or tract of land of some size, somewhere in the circle of the empire. Indeed, it is said that even the artisans and laborers in the towns and villages are almost invariably the owners

of a plot of land, sometimes even in remote quarters of Russia.
This fact constitutes one of the impediments to a more rapid and general development of the manufacturing and industrial interests of Russia. The agricultural element so vastly predominating over the urban, necessitates a reliance upon the rural population to supply the needed labor in the factories. The devotion of the peasant to his humble holding of land, to which he invariably returns at stated seasons to cultivate, thus abandoning his position as an artisan, prevents that permanent organization of labor so needful to secure success in manufacturing and commercial enterprises.

This exceptional feature of peasant life finds, in some measure, a solution in the condition of this class prior to the emancipation act of Alexander II. in 1861.

Previous to that great epoch the peasants were entirely the serfs of either the state, the crown, or the nobility, to whom they stood in a relation of the closest personal dependence. Of the whole peasant or serf class, there was, at that time, something like 11,000,000 families, of which about forty-six per cent. belonged respectively each to the state and the nobility—or private persons—and about eight per cent. to the crown. Those who lived on the lands of the nobility were usually permitted to cultivate a tract of land at their own expense, out of which they derived their subsistence, and it became known as the peasant lot. Beyond this necessary labor, he was bound to work under the direction, control, and for the sole benefit of the landlord, who possessed the legal right, under vague limitations, to dispose of the person and property of the peasant. Thus, by the sanction of custom and long usage, there dawned that first peasant proprietary right or usufruct, which under the benign rescript of 1861 suddenly brightened into the full day of individual freedom and property right. By this act of emancipation, not only was the obligatory relation of dependence of peasant to owner absolved, but it also provided for a compulsory redemption of the lands of the nobility or private owners occupied under the former shadowy rights of the peasants. Not at once, however, were these lands redeemed, as by an agreement between the interested parties the peasants were allowed to occupy their former holdings of the lands of their old masters by the payment of an annual rental, which land the government apportioned to them, becoming inalienable.

The same arrangement was made respecting the peasants that belonged to the state and the crown, except that such peasants were not obliged, under the proclamation, to begin the redemption of their lands until 1885, while for those peasants who were the property of private parties the date was fixed at 1881. To carry into practical effect this obligatory redemption of lands, the government issued its bonds to the old land-owners to an amount estimated on the rental value of the lands. This debt was to be liquidated by the peasants in the course of forty-nine years, by annual instalments of principal and interest.

To facilitate this redemption measure, state peasant banks were founded, which loaned money to the peasants on easy terms, taking a mortgage on the lands as a security. It might be further stated that the lands were allotted to the males only, and without regard to age, and largely to the communes, which were at the same time given the amplest powers of local self-government.

To aid in forming some just idea of the scope of this memorable act, and the stupendous changes wrought by it, I will briefly collate a few facts and figures that official statistics supply. For convenience, I will divide the lands that passed under this proclamation into three classes or groups, viz.: those that comprise holdings from two to seven acres, those from seven to seventeen acres, and those from eighteen to over forty acres.

We find that an allotment of lands from two to

seven acres was made to 6,280,000 males, aggregating in the total 37,800,000 acres. Of this number of peasants, 4,833,300 were formerly those belonging to private parties, and the remainder, 1,447,000, those belonging to the crown and the state. Out of the total allotment of 37,800,000 acres, 27,800,000 acres went to the peasants formerly belonging to private parties, averaging about five and a half acres per male, while 10,000,000 acres went to the former peasants of the crown and state, averaging nearly seven acres per male.

For the second class—that is, allotments of seven to seventeen acres—there was granted 154,171,800 acres, distributed among 12,400,000 males, or an average of 12.4 acres per capita. Of the total number of serfs who fell within this group under this class, 5,572,200 were those that belonged to private parties, and 6,830,000 that were owned by the crown and the state. To the former were allotted 64,320,200 acres, or nearly twelve acres per capita, and to the latter nearly 90,000,000 acres, or a per capita holding of about thirteen acres. In the third class—from eighteen to over forty acres—we find there were 3,714,390 males, and an aggregate of 124,979,000 acres, or 33.4 per male. Of the total serf or private class in this group, 3,369,600 were owned by the state and the crown, to whom was alloted 115,979,000 acres, or an average of thirty-four acres to each male. The peasants that had been held by private parties in this class were 344,796, to whom were granted 8,666,000 acres, or nearly twenty-five acres as an average to each male.

To summarize, we find that there was a male population of something over 22,000,000, to whom under the rescript of 1861 there were allotted 316,200,000 acres, or an average of nearly fifteen acres for each. Of the grand total of serfs manumitted by that act, 10,800,000, or nearly one-half, were those of private owners. The other half, excepting the small number owned by the church and monasteries, was the property of the state and the crown.

The lands, therefore, for the obligatory redemption of which the government provided by the issuance of its bonds, amounted to a trifle over 100,000,000 acres, or somewhat less than one-third of all the lands transferred by this act, being an average of a little less than ten acres per capita. There were, therefore, left of the state and crown lands about 215,000,000 acres, to be apportioned among something over 11,000,000 holdings, or about twenty acres per capita.

Very naturally, some notable results followed a change in condition so fundamental and at the same time so rapid, and it speaks well for the sterling qualities and character of this great class that a transformation so swift and radical carried with it so little confusion and disorder. The usual desire to accumulate speedily grew up among a people who hitherto were without property, when they found themselves suddenly endowed with such a substantial evidence of wealth as land. As a result, the peasantry of Russia, since the act of 1861, have added by purchase to their holdings acquired under that act, over 50,000,000 acres, so that they now hold some 370,000,000 acres, or, as before stated, over one-third of the arable acreage of European Russia.

One of the direct results of this newly created and extensive ownership of lands is that the conflict between capital and labor exists to a less degree in this country, perhaps, than in any other. As the land acquired by the peasant is as a rule not sufficient in itself to consume his whole labor or yield a full support to himself and family, he is therefore compelled to repair this deficiency by seeking service under the owner of a larger estate, in some factory or other occupation.

Having become a land-owner himself, however, and therefore receiving in some degree a reward for his labor through his own capital, he thus stands in quite a different relation to one whose employment he seeks, than the laborer who derives his reward for services wholly from the capital of another. This necessity on the part of the peasant to supplement the labor on his own insufficient tract of land by employment elsewhere, causes a movement among the rural classes which, if not rightly understood, might lead to a very erroneous impression.

The almost incredible number of peasants that one meets on all lines of travel in this country at certain seasons of the year would seem to indicate that they were a very uneasy, shifting, and discontented class. But this is not true, since almost the entire migratory movements of this class arise out of a quest for employment elsewhere than on their own inadequate lot or tract of land, to which they invariably return with punctual regularity at certain times and seasons, as they are devoted to their little lot of land, and they allow nothing to separate them for long from it. Even when some poor peasant—as it often occurs—acquires wealth in some distant place as a merchant, or in other pursuits, and becomes the owner of buildings and other property in a city, he invariably retains his membership in the commune from whence he came, and he clings to his little holding of land there ; for, as he says, his lot of land cannot be taken from him, and it would afford him and his children a living should he chance to lose his accumulated wealth.

It is only when a peasant emigrates to some distant province that he permanently severs the bond that binds him to the little lot acquired under the emancipation act of 1861. Indeed, I was informed by those connected with the movement for the settlement of the new lands in Siberia and elsewhere, that the tenacity with which the peasant adheres to his tract of land was one of the obstacles in the way of emigration to the new and distant lands, and that it was no uncommon thing for a peasant to voluntarily abandon larger and better holdings in new countries and return again to his little lot in the old commune.

This firm attachment of so large a class to the lands of the country, and the fact that five-sixths of her population are engaged in the simple, invigorating, and healthful pursuit of agriculture, conducing to a sound national vitality and energy, is a circumstance not to be lost sight of in considering what Russia's future is to be, in the possible clash of nations that may be precipitated some day by the pressure and necessities of a population existing under the highly artificial, intricate, and transitory conditions of an urban life.

EMANCIPATION CARRIED INTO EFFECT

It was on February 19, 1861, over two months prior to the outbreak of civil war in America, and nearly two years before our own great Lincoln issued his emancipation proclamation, that the memorable rescript of the Czar Alexander II. flashed through the long night of Russian serfdom and upon the world, bringing immediate freedom to an enslaved class almost one-half greater in number than the entire population of the whole United States at that time, both slave and free. By a wise and humane foresight, there were, also, provisions embodied in this very act to enable a hitherto dependent class to speedily become, in a measure, self-sustaining, and in other ways to assume the burdens, duties, and obligations created by their newly acquired rights and condition. Thus it was that we see a complete reversal of the old order of things, the serfs becoming the owners of the lands they occupied and for the use of which they served their masters, which lands, in turn, under this decree, the masters were compelled to apportion among their former serfs, creating thereby what is, perhaps, the largest single body of land-owners on the globe.

When we consider that the serf system was the growth of centuries, and had become intimately interwoven in every fibre of the political, social, and economic institutions and traditions of Russia; and, further, that the purposes contemplated by the act have been realized in the fullest measure, without drawing a sword or firing a gun, it deservedly stands as the most remarkable achievement in the interests of humanity ever accomplished by a ruler or a nation.

Thirty-seven years later we find the head of this great nation, the grandson of the serf-freeing Czar, again startling the world by the issuance of another rescript, making for the peace and weal of the world in a no less remarkable manner. Let us hope that the success attending the benign efforts of his great predecessor will crown the efforts of the present ruler. With these examples before us, despite a prejudice that may exist against this people—the cause of which can only be suspected —one finds himself irresistibly impelled to seriously inquire what manner of nation, after all, this really is, that it should so far anticipate all others by voluntarily taking the initiative in measures calculated to so profoundly effect and promote the freedom, peace, and welfare of the human race.

IV

Stations and restaurants on Siberian railway—Equipment and safety of road—Syzran on the Volga River—The Tartar—Bridge on Siberian railway over the Volga River—The Volga, its size and importance as a highway—First view of the Ural Mountains—Their height, etc.—The city of Zlatoust—Government works and mines in the Ural Mountains—Summit of the Urals—Entrance into Siberia—Some facts concerning the Russian Empire—Eastern slope of the Ural Mountains—Crop conditions in the Volga valley—A look ahead.

THE Siberian railway, like all railways in Russia, is well constructed, the road-bed firm, track well ballasted, generally with stone, at least as far as Tscheljabinsk, and easy gradients. The road has a five-foot gauge, uniform with all the roads in European Russia. This gives an ample breadth to the cars, which, with their unusual height, imparts an air of comfort not possessed by roads of narrower gauge and less height of ceiling in the car. The stations, without exception, are clean and handsome, constructed often of wood, but frequently of brick or stone. It is a perfect delight to take a meal in the restaurants. They have a most agreeable custom of furnishing meals. On entering the dining-room, you will find at one end an immense sideboard literally groaning under a load of newly prepared Russian dishes, always piping hot, and of such a bewildering variety as to range through the whole gamut of human fancy and tastes.

You are given a plate, with a knife and fork. Making your own selection, you retire to any of the neatly-spread tables to enjoy your meal at your leisure, and, I might add, with infinite zest, for travel in this country, besides pleasing the eye, quickens the palate. The price, too, is a surprise to one accustomed to metropolitan charges. You can get soup, as fine a beefsteak as you ever ate, a splendid roast chicken, whole, done in Russian style, most toothsome and juicy; potatoes and other vegetables, a bottle of beer, splendid and brewed in this country, for one ruble—about fifty cents.

Safety seems to be the one idea uppermost in the minds of the railway ministry. Beside the electrical and other appliances used in the best railway practice, they have an immense army of guards both for the train and the track. The road is divided into sections of one verst each—about two-thirds of a mile. For each section there is built a neat little cottage in which the guard and his family live. It is the duty of this guard or one of his family to patrol a section night and day. As soon as a train passes, the guard steps into the middle of the track, holds a flag—at night a lantern—aloft and watches the retreating train until it passes into the next verst or section. Where there is a heavy curve that prevents the view of the road for the distance of a verst, several guards are employed

SYZRAN ON THE VOLGA RIVER

on a section. A train is, therefore, never out of sight of a guard.

I might add that women often perform this service, which is quite apart from that of the section gang, whose duty is to repair the road. On the

Siberian railway, as far as Tomsk, there are to be nearly 4,000 of these cottages for the use of the guards; a very costly precaution, but one that gives a pleasing sense of security to the traveller. With the exception of the great post routes to Siberia, the Caucasus, and main highways in European Russia, which are first class and compare well with other countries, the common roads of Russia are indifferent, scarcely equal to those of our own country.

On leaving Moscow, there are no towns worthy of being called cities excepting at long intervals, but farm villages are passed with rapid frequency, since of the immense farming class, as I have stated, none dwell on the farms they cultivate, but live wholly in villages or communes. The first town that is possessed of especial interest is Syzran, in the valley of the Volga. It is the centre of an immense grain trade, since it is surrounded by one of the best and richest cereal-growing regions in East Russia. There are celebrated tanneries there.

Here, also, one discovers in feature and quaint costume the first traces of the true Tartar, which, at Samara, 100 miles on, develops into a distinct class and pronounced type. On looking at these tawny and grizzled representatives of a once powerful race, the mind reverts to the mighty warriors that, from Attila down, swept like a blighting

SAMARA ON THE VOLGA RIVER

scourge over Asia and Europe, leaving a Tartar trail even on the steppes of Russia.

At Batraki, another important grain port, and

BATRAKI ON THE VOLGA

celebrated for the fine quality of caviare, the railroad crosses the Volga. The bridge here, owing to its immense size and the difficulties encountered in its construction, deserves well to be classed among the world's great structures of this kind.

It is only a little short of a mile in length, being built of fourteen sections, 360 feet span each. The bridge is 135 feet above the river at low water. There were consumed nearly 7,000 tons of iron in its building, and it was designed and executed by a Russian engineer.

The Volga also well merits being ranked among the great rivers of the world. It is navigable for over 2,000 miles, and to within a few hundred miles of St. Petersburg, as it takes a semicircular sweep from the northwest towards Nijni Novgorod, and thence in a general southeastern direction to the Caspian Sea, which it enters at Astrakhan. A canal has been constructed from Ladoga Sea to Rybinsk, the head of the navigation of the Volga, so that vessels can go from the Baltic down the Volga to the Caspian Sea, thus cutting right through middle European Russia, bisecting it by a waterway of over 2,500 miles.

The Volga, where we crossed it, very much resembles the Mississippi River, as well in size as in other points. To form some notion of the size and volume of water in this mighty river, I would say, at the point where the railroad crosses the river it is just a mile wide at low water. At times of high water it is from four to eight miles wide. The channel near the bridge at low water has a depth of twenty feet, and at high water of 100 feet.

GREAT BRIDGE ACROSS THE VOLGA RIVER AT BATRAKI ON THE TRANS-SIBERIAN RAILWAY

The velocity of the current when the river is at its flood is said to be thirty feet per second, and in its low stage, fifteen or twenty feet per second.

From Batraki to Wajsaowaja, a distance of 500

RUSSIAN VILLAGE ON THE UFA RIVER

miles, there are the same fertile treeless plains and prairies as from Moscow to the former place, a distance of 600 miles. At Wajsaowaja we encounter the foot-hills and get our first view of the Ural Mountains. We here also meet the Ufa

River, whose sinuous course the road follows until the summit of the mountains is reached.

Those who from its great length—being over 1,700 miles from north to south—have been led

FIRST VIEW OF THE URAL MOUNTAINS AFTER PASSING WAJSAO-WAJA, TRANS-SIBERIAN RAILWAY

to expect an imposing range of mountains, will be doomed to disappointment. The height is only moderate, being a little over 6,000 feet at the highest, in this respect scarcely equal to the

Apennines. The summit is reached a little beyond Zlatoust, at an elevation of 3,000 feet. It is an easy grade and requires no special effort to surmount.

On reaching the summit, if one did not know it

THE WESTERN SLOPE OF THE URAL MOUNTAINS ON THE TRANS-SIBERIAN RAILWAY, BETWEEN UFA AND ZLATOUST

was the Ural Mountains, he might well believe he was on the railway summit of the Alleghanies near Altoona, so similar to it are the surroundings. Zlatoust, a large town, is most important in several particulars. It was until recently the "Botany Bay" of Russia. Here one occasionally sees prisoners chained in gangs destined to work in the mines or perhaps, doomed to the solitude of farther Siberia.

Zlatoust is in the centre of the iron regions of Russia. A very fine quality is produced here in

STATION AT ZLATOUST ON TRANS-SIBERIAN RAILWAY NEAR THE SUMMIT OF THE URAL MOUNTAINS

great quantities, and being free from both sulphur and phosphorus, it is consumed principally in making sheets and bars for those purposes where the highest quality is required.

The region to the northward, extending to Perm and Ekaterinburg, abounds in gold, copper, mala-

MANUFACTURE OF FIREARMS

chite, lapis-lazuli, and other precious metals and minerals, all of which are being extensively mined and worked. At the former place, which is located on the Kama River, there are immense government works, employing over 2,000 men. It has one of

MONUMENT ON SUMMIT OF URAL MOUNTAINS INDICATING DIVIDING
LINE BETWEEN EUROPE AND ASIA

the largest steam hammers in the world, and the foundry turns out steel cannon of unusual size and quality. They also manufacture firearms here, said to equal anything manufactured in Europe or America, and sidearms of unsurpassed excellence. It is from these localities in the Ural Mountains that what is known in America as "Russian iron" comes.

In Zlatoust, also, there are great government

EASTERN SLOPE OF THE URAL MOUNTAINS ON THE TRANS-SIBERIAN RAILWAY, MIDWAY BETWEEN ZLATOUST AND TSCHELJABINSK

works for the manufacture of steel cannon and other arms. Cutlery of various kinds is made in large quantities, and it is said the swords are of exceptional quality. There are also produced marvellous castings from pig-iron. The statuettes cast out of this metal are marvels of artistic beauty and technical skill. Their quality, it is said, is due largely to the superior moulding sand produced in this region, but I am of the impression that it is

EASTERN SLOPE OF URAL MOUNTAINS ON TRANS-SIBERIAN RAILWAY, EIGHTY MILES FROM THE SUMMIT OF THE URAL MOUNTAINS

more properly attributable to the rare qualities of the iron, which seems to flow with unusual fluidity, producing castings so delicate in detail as to be scarcely distinguishable from bronze. These art products are rapidly finding their way into European markets.

The town is located on a pretty little lake nestled most picturesquely among the hills, almost on the summit of the range.

Shortly after leaving Zlatoust we pass a large

ON TRANS-SIBERIAN RAILWAY JUST BEFORE ARRIVING AT TSCHELJABINSK

stone monument erected at some distance from the railway. On one side is, in Russian, the word "Europe," and on the opposite side "Asia." It marks the boundary between Europe and Asia. One, however, does not need a monumental token to learn that he is passing from one great geographical division to another, for the sparse population, uncultivated lands, and general wild aspect only too clearly indicate that he has suddenly entered Siberia.

Here a few facts may aid the imagination. The Russian Empire contains a little over one-seventh of the land surface of the entire globe, and about one-twenty-fifth of its whole surface. European Russia, with Poland and Finland included, has two million square miles, with over one hundred millions of people. The Central Asian provinces, with the Caucasus, Merv, and Kars, has 1,500,000 square miles, and 14,000,000 people. Siberia contains nearly 5,000,000 square miles and a population of only 4,000,000. When we reflect that its area is nearly three times that of Europe, which has over 200,000,000 people, it is a matter of no great surprise that one quickly detects his advent into this empty country.

The eastern slope of the Ural Mountains is, for a space, more abrupt than the western, but it soon enters upon a gentle slope that continues until it touches the western edge of that great level plain which seems to stretch indefinitely to the east. On leaving the summit we join the Isset, a small river, whose course we closely follow until it deflects to the northeast, becoming a tributary to the Irtish, itself one of the main branches of the great Obi River. Fifty miles farther on in the plains we come to Tscheljabinsk, where ends the first section of this great railway.

It may not be amiss to give the results of my

RAILWAY STATION AT TSCHELJABINSK, THE END OF THE FIRST SECTION OF TRANS-SIBERIAN RAILWAY, AT THE EASTERN FOOT OF URAL MOUNTAINS.

observations respecting this year's crop conditions in the country through which I have passed, constituting as it does the finest cereal region in all European Russia. From a deficiency in rainfall, extending continuously over a period of almost four months, an alarming shortage of all crops, even grass, is certain to exist throughout an immense area, reaching through several hundred miles east and west, and perhaps five hundred miles north and

ENTERING THE PLAINS OR STEPPES OF SIBERIA ON THE TRANS-SIBERIAN RAILWAY, ONE HUNDRED MILES EAST OF THE URAL MOUNTAINS

south — an area about equally bisected by the Volga River and the railway line throughout this vast tract. This includes five of the largest and agriculturally the most important governments of Russia, containing from ten to twelve million people, and it is almost certain that enough cannot be raised this year to meet the wants of more than one-fourth of its population.

The government of Samara (said to be twice as large as Belgium) lies in the centre of the stricken

CROSSING THE SIBERIAN STEPPES, TWO HUNDRED MILES EAST OF THE URAL MOUNTAINS, ON THE SIBERIAN RAILWAY

region, and here already much distress has developed. I learn, on passing through, that the Czar has just given 500,000 rubles for the relief of the sufferers. The region over which the drought extends is the finest wheat region in Eastern Russia,

KIRGHIZ TARTAR AUL OR VILLAGE ON SIBERIAN STEPPES.

and in ordinary seasons supplies a large surplus for export to foreign countries. I was informed by a Russian official connected with the ministry of railways, that they would probably have to bring into this region where the shortage has occurred, from other sections of Russia, from fifty to eighty million bushels of grain, to supply the necessary food to the inhabitants and seed to the farmers. The self-sustaining power of this great empire is fully made manifest by the fact that while so serious a shortage has occurred in one great section, in many others, such as the Crimea, the Caucasus, and the newly settled lands in Siberia, abundant and even excessive crops are reported, so that not only can the deficit be fully supplied from her own home resources, but there will be left over a fair surplus for export.

The foregoing, however, only tends to bring into stronger relief the fact that year by year the once wide margin between supply and demand in the food products of the world is gradually being narrowed, and suggests some uncomfortable reflections as to what might result if, instead of many years of yield much above the average, as it has been during the past ten years, the world should be called upon to meet years of average production—quite as probable a contingency—to say nothing of the possibility of years of continuous deficiency.

As my objective point lies somewhat over 2,000 miles east of this, and less than 200 miles from the northern China border, and as it has to be performed by taking slow and uncertain railway trains,

VIEW ACROSS SIBERIAN STEPPES, THREE HUNDRED MILES EAST OF THE URAL MOUNTAINS

not to say exhausting troikas, you can form some notion of the wearisome journey I have in prospect. I have long since learned, however, that nothing well worth can be achieved without corresponding outlay of energy. As the Macedonian pikeman said in answer to an inquiry why he was content to follow the Grecian commander on his fatiguing conquests, "If you take no pains, you get no gains."

I shall probably write you from Tomsk, about

GROUP OF KIRGHIZ TARTARS AT STATION ON SIBERIAN RAILWAY

twelve hundred miles east of this. It may be several days, however, as I shall probably tarry some on the way. The railway line runs over 1,200 miles right through the domain of the Kirghiz, the most interesting of all the Tartars, and a most important character to study. I am informed that they are yet the same untamed nomads that, under Mondzuk and his successors, as a mongrel Tartar and Mongol horde, swept with such destructive fury nearly 1,600 years ago through the length and breadth of Europe, holding even Rome in terror for several centuries.

ON SIBERIAN STEPPES, THREE HUNDRED AND FIFTY MILES EAST OF URAL MOUNTAINS

ON SIBERIAN STEPPES, EIGHT HUNDRED MILES EAST OF URAL MOUNTAINS

V

The Asiatic continent—A glance at Siberia, its geography, physical characteristics, etc.—The great rivers of Siberia—Erroneous impression of Siberia—Vast area of level land—No difficulty in construction of railway—Similarity of Western Siberia to a great portion of the United States—The error of Americans respecting trans-Missouri River country—The route of the Siberian railway—Its construction and equipment—Stations on railway in Siberia—Track, bridges, etc.—Accumulated grain on the route from Kurgan to Tomsk—The necessity for increased facilities on Siberian railway—Flora and fauna of Siberia—Agricultural resources of Siberia—Possibilities of the country.

TOMSK, *August*, 1898.

MAGNITUDES and distances are pitched to such a huge scale on this mammoth Asiatic continent that one must needs fortify himself by constant reference to maps and charts in order to maintain his bearings, and even to know his whereabouts. If you will refer to your map, you will see that this is north of Burmah and quite on the longitude of Calcutta, and is nearly 1,800 miles east of the Caspian Sea and well at the middle of the northern border of the great Chinese Empire, from which it is distant only about 400 miles.

To aid in forming an intelligible understanding

of the country through which I have passed, and of the railway that traverses it, a brief glance at the main geographic and physical characteristics

VIEW ACROSS THE IRTISH RIVER, SIBERIA

of Siberia may, I believe, properly be made. Our maps show us that Siberia is a vast country of nearly 5,000,000 square miles area, extending from the northern confines of China and Turkestan to the Arctic Sea, through over thirty degrees of

STATION ON SIBERIAN RAILWAY, FOUR HUNDRED MILES EAST OF URAL MOUNTAINS

latitude, and, from the Ural Mountains in the west to the Pacific Ocean in the east, through about 130 degrees of longitude. Truly, this is a country of "magnificent distances."

In substantially parallel courses there are many

VIEW ACROSS THE ISHIM RIVER, SIBERIA

mighty rivers flowing through the entire breadth of Siberia into the Northern Sea. The chief ones are the Obi, the Yenisei, and the Lena. The main stems of these rivers usually extend southward 1,000 or 1,200 miles, when by numerous radiating tributaries they spread fan-like through an immense area of country, finally finding their source in the great, high plateaus of Central Asia. The railway line, therefore, in its western half

ON THE TOM RIVER, SIBERIA

passes through the upper reaches of the Obi and the Yenisei rivers.

Somehow I had formed the idea that Siberia was, in the main, a mountainous, broken, barren, and even sterile country, covered with forests— which opinion, I am inclined to think, is some-

NEW SETTLEMENT ON OPEN STEPPES OF SIBERIA, SIX HUNDRED MILES EAST OF URAL MOUNTAINS

what generally entertained in the west. Nothing could be farther from the fact. Of all the sur-

ON SIBERIAN STEPPES OR PRAIRIES, FOUR HUNDRED AND FIFTY MILES EAST OF THE URAL MOUNTAINS

prises met with in my somewhat extensive travels, Siberia is the greatest.

As a whole, it contains perhaps the largest continuous area of level lands on the globe. Excepting spurs of the great Altai range of mountains fringing its southern border, and which cut occasionally to some distance northward into Siberia, the entire western half of the country is exceptionally level, almost to flatness. Near Lake Baikal, in the foot-hills of the Altais, the moun-

ON SIBERIAN STEPPES, BETWEEN KURGAN AND PETROPAVLOVSK

tains rise to a height of not over 6,000 feet; and it is only when going 100 miles farther, to the very China border, that anything like a great altitude is reached.

The railway, therefore, having no great mountain ranges to cross, and throughout almost its

TWO VIEWS ACROSS SIBERIAN STEPPES

entire length being built through a practically level country, presents no example of more than ordinary engineering achievement; in fact, it will be no more difficult to construct it clear through to the Pacific Ocean than it was to build the Union Pacific from Omaha to Salt Lake City.

If a great section of country of the United States and British America be taken, extending from the Gulf of Mexico through thirty degrees of latitude northward, and 2,000 miles eastward from the Rocky Mountains, it would fairly represent an area of country similar in physical characteristics to that portion of Siberia which we are considering. Indeed, the resemblance is not in extent only, for in their geological formation they are quite identical—the one being formed by the wash in primeval times from the eastern escarpment of the Rocky Mountains, and the other from the northern face of the great Central Asian mountains in the south and that of the Urals in the west. The alluvial character of the soil in both places goes far to bear out this identity of origin.

This general similarity, I am sure, will hold for the western half of Siberia and that region in the United States lying between the Rocky and Alleghany mountains. It would not be far from the fact to say that for 2,000 miles east of the Ural Mountains, and extending to the Arctic Sea,

Siberia is almost as level as the ocean. In over 1,000 miles I do not believe the grade of the railroad varied 300 feet, and in many places it was as straight as an arrow, without the slightest

VIEW ACROSS SIBERIAN STEPPES, FIVE HUNDRED MILES EAST OF THE URAL MOUNTAINS

curve for forty or fifty miles. Indeed, there was one stretch of perfectly straight road for 116 versts, or nearly eighty miles.

It is somewhat difficult to obtain specific information of the geography and geology of this region or even of the real nature of the soil. The Russians, even of the intelligent and often of the official class, possess generally only a superficial knowledge of the great country they have so suddenly brought to the eyes of the world.

In this respect they much resemble the eastern residents of our own country, whose geographers and scientists fifty years ago regarded the trans-Mississippi River region as a *terra incognita*, and insisted on recording in the maps of those days as the "Great American Desert" the whole region west of the Missouri River, now the most fertile and fruitful country in the whole United States.

For the real nature of the soil, its capacity, etc., I rely much on careful observation and such information as I can extract from the Kirghiz, who come to the railway from hundreds of miles both north and south. The Russian government is making rapid and extensive surveys, and I doubt not at no distant day will supply the world with much specific knowledge of this hitherto almost unknown land.

The railway on leaving Tscheljabinsk takes an almost due easterly course, which it varies by a few points only until beyond the Yenisei River, a distance of about 2,000 miles, when it deflects to the southeast for nearly 800 miles, until it reaches

Lake Baikal, only a short distance from the China border. It follows somewhat closely the old post route from Moscow to Irkutsk, running via Zlatoust, where at Tomsk it joins the more northern post route down the Tobol and Irtish

KIRGHIZ TARTARS AND CAMEL TRAIN ON SIBERIAN STEPPES

rivers to Tiumen, and thence over the Ural Mountains to Perm and Nijni Novgorod to Moscow.

Curiously enough, the railway follows much the same course as that by which in ancient times the Huns, Tartars, and Moguls made through Southern Russia their numerous and dreaded incursions into Europe.

RAILWAY BRIDGE OVER THE OBI RIVER ON SIBERIAN RAILWAY

EQUIPMENT EQUAL TO UNION PACIFIC 91

A sufficiently accurate general description of the Siberian railroad and its various appointments would, I think, be covered by the statement that

RAILWAY STATION ON SIBERIAN RAILWAY, EIGHT HUNDRED MILES EAST OF URAL MOUNTAINS, OR OVER TWO THOUSAND MILES EAST OF MOSCOW

it is fully equal to either the Union or Northern Pacific Railway, although the oldest portion east of Tscheljabinsk has been in operation scarcely two years, and the newer portions a few months only.

The track is well laid, the grading firm and thorough, and the bridges almost wholly of iron, save a few of the original and temporary ones, which are rapidly being replaced by those of

STATION ON SIBERIAN RAILWAY

stone and iron. Those over the Irtish, Ishim, Obi, Tobol, Omsk, and Tom rivers I found to be well constructed, of the best material and most approved modern pattern.

The stations, always artistic and picturesque,

and never of the same style, are neat, comfortable, of good size, and substantial, fully equal to the average depot on the New York Central or Penn-

SACKED GRAIN AWAITING SHIPMENT AT THE STATION ON SIBERIAN RAILWAY BETWEEN OMSK AND TOMSK, OVER ONE THOUSAND MILES EAST OF THE URAL MOUNTAINS.

sylvania. I noticed that recent surveys have been made along the line, and on inquiry was informed that they are preparing to build one or more additional tracks. This is a very timely provision, as the road is already taxed far beyond its capacity.

All along the line I saw piles of grain and other

PASSENGER TRAIN FOR ORDINARY SERVICE ON TRANS-SIBERIAN RAILWAY, MAKING DAILY TRIPS TO TOMSK, NEARLY THREE THOUSAND MILES EAST OF MOSCOW

kinds of freight awaiting shipment. One of the officials of the road informed me that there were over 8,000,000 bushels of wheat lying at the depots between Kurgan and Tomsk, which could not be carried. The road is crowded with emigrant trains eastward, and this, with the development of the country on the line and the carrying of the material for thousands of miles of road yet

VIEW ON THE SIBERIAN STEPPES, BETWEEN THE TOBOL AND ISHIM RIVERS. EMIGRANT TRAIN CROSSING THE STEPPES TO OCCUPY NEW LANDS

to be built beyond, has naturally enough brought about a serious block in traffic.

To those familiar with the rapid growth and development of the trans-Missouri River region and the traffic necessities it created, it is apparent that in a few years this great highway will have to increase its present facilities several times over.

ON THE OPEN STEPPES OF SIBERIA, ABOUT ONE THOUSAND MILES EAST OF THE URAL MOUNTAINS, OR NEARLY TWO THOUSAND FOUR HUNDRED MILES EAST OF MOSCOW

In addition to the trade and travel that must result from binding commercially and socially together 500,000,000 people in the Far East and 300,000,000 in the West, there will be that due to the devel-

FLORA AND FAUNA OF SIBERIA

opment of an intermediate country, in combined fertility and extent far surpassing anything yet undeveloped on the globe.

To describe in full and satisfactory detail the flora, fauna, fertility of soil, and the various re-

VIEW ACROSS SIBERIAN PRAIRIES

sources of this wonderful country would transcend the limits of time and space of a letter. It would require volumes to do this. I will, therefore, have to confine myself to generalities merely. I have already said that there lies in Western Siberia, from the Ural Mountains eastward, an unbroken tract of practically level land, about 800 miles wide and nearly 2,000 miles long; that is to say, an area equal to two-thirds of the United States, excepting Alaska.

When I add that for the most part it is like or

DISTANT HERD OF CATTLE ON SIBERIAN PLAINS OR STEPPES

even superior to the fertile, treeless, level prairies of our own great West; that it extends over thirty degrees of latitude, from the genial climate of Central Asia to the frigid north; that throughout this vast region is to be found the finest pasturage in the world; that in many parts wheat and other cereals can be grown equal to the Dakotas or Minnesota, and even Indian corn over a large

EMIGRANTS AT RAILWAY STATION BETWEEN KAINSK AND TOMSK ON THE TRANS-SIBERIAN RAILWAY

region in the south—some feeble conception can be formed of the tremendous latent agricultural resources of this country.

This fact is emphasized by the further statement that it is inhabited by only a comparatively small population of Tartars and other nomadic tribes. The cities being few and small, the fixed population is relatively insignificant.

For the whole of Siberia there is less than one person to the square mile. If it be further added, that this country lies practically between the same degrees of latitude as European Russia; that it has an area much greater and an average fertility of soil even superior in many places; and that the latter country already supports over 100,000,000 of people, with a liberal surplus, some notion may be formed of the teeming millions that are yet to people this waste land, when it is made available by an adequate railway system and other means of intercommunication and transportation, which, under the newly awakened spirit of Russian enterprise, seems destined to be accomplished in due time. Indeed, a most comprehensive system has already crystallized into something of a concrete form.

NEW SETTLEMENT ON SIBERIAN RAILWAY, ONE THOUSAND MILES EAST OF THE URAL MOUNTAINS

VI

Ultimate Siberian railway system—Proposed line from Central Siberia to Persian Gulf—New relations between Russia and China, arising from the Siberian railway—Change from the route as originally projected—New route to Vladivostok—Rapid settlement of country on Siberian railway—Quick growth of towns on the line—Development of lands to follow railway extension—Grazing lands on Siberian railway—Small lakes through Siberia—Timber in Western Siberia.

I was fortunate enough to form the acquaintance of one of the engineers of the Siberian railway, a most courteous gentleman, who gave me not only many details concerning the great line, but also a brief outline of the proposed ultimate Siberian system. In addition to the contemplated line running northward to Tobolsk and several toward the China border, they design running one in a southwestern direction toward Samarkand, crossing the trans-Caspian road, now completed to the western border of China, and thence southward through Persia, with its ultimate destination on the Persian Gulf.

The recent *entente* with China has caused a radical change in the plan of the eastern section of the Siberian railway, as originally projected. Instead of making the long detour via the Amoor River to Vladivostok, necessitated by passing

VIEW ACROSS THE SIBERIAN STEPPES, NINE HUNDRED MILES EAST OF THE URAL MOUNTAINS, OR ABOUT TWO THOUSAND TWO HUNDRED MILES EAST OF MOSCOW

around Manchuria, they are now permitted, under the new treaty with China, to construct a line running through that province direct to Vladivostok.

RAILWAY IN MANCHURIA 105

They have, therefore, stopped work for the present on the eastern section of the line, and are bending all their energies to build, in the

RECENT SETTLEMENT ON SIBERIAN RAILWAY, ONE THOUSAND ONE HUNDRED MILES EAST OF URAL MOUNTAINS.

shortest possible time, a line through Manchuria to their newly acquired open port on the China Sea, at Port Arthur. This line will leave the main one at Chiti, about 800 miles east of Lake

Baikal, following almost a due east course to Vladivostok.

A line will branch off at Kirin and run due south to Port Arthur. This will create a system that will make Russian influence practically paramount in Manchuria.

A prominent Russian gentleman, residing at Vladivostok, who was on the train on his way over the proposed route, spoke very freely of the intentions of his government in that quarter, substantially confirming the plans given me by the engineer of the line. Under this newly revised scheme, the route to Vladivostok will be shortened many hundreds of miles from that originally projected.

All along the route of the Siberian railway are to be found those examples of quick settlement of country and sudden growth of towns so familiar in Iowa, Kansas, and Nebraska in the early days of the extension of railways through those States. Every few miles a station is located on the open plains or prairies, around which there quickly clusters a thriving village. Fields of newly cultivated lands, many covered with a golden harvest, can be seen for miles at all these stations. There are some instances of rapid growth not surpassed in our own great West.

After crossing the Obi River, we stopped at a

RECENT SETTLEMENT ON SIBERIAN RAILWAY, NINE HUNDRED AND FIFTY MILES EAST OF URAL MOUNTAINS

town called Obb, of over 14,000 inhabitants, containing many handsome buildings and several beautiful church edifices. It was a flourishing

NEW SETTLEMENT ON SIBERIAN RAILWAY, TWO THOUSAND FIVE HUNDRED MILES EAST OF MOSCOW, BETWEEN OBB AND TOMSK

community and the seat of an active trade. I was told that less than three years ago there was not a house existing where the town now stands, and, indeed, that the whole country around was one of wild solitude and desolation.

With these accomplished results before us, it is easy to see what a magical transformation must take place in this great country under the influence of an extended railway system. It is all the more

NEW SETTLEMENT ON TRANS-SIBERIAN RAILWAY, ONE THOUSAND ONE HUNDRED MILES EAST OF THE URALS, AND BETWEEN KRIWOSTCHE-KOWO AND KAINSK.

easily imagined by one who has already seen in his own country an object lesson of a similar character. I doubt if the Russians fully realize to what an extent their great enterprise is going to modify their economic and, perhaps, social conditions.

CHURCH IN NEW TOWN OF OBB

FUTURE DEVELOPMENT OF COUNTRY 113

For reasons I will hereafter give, this great region is not likely to be settled and developed with that rapidity which marked our lightning-like

NEW SETTLEMENT ON SIBERIAN RAILWAY, ONE THOUSAND TWO HUNDRED AND FIFTY MILES EAST OF THE URALS, OR ABOUT TWO THOUSAND FIVE HUNDRED MILES EAST OF MOSCOW

advance in the West; still it will be fast enough to make a decided change in the commercial and economic interests of old or European Russia, unsettling for a time to some extent—as it did in our country—the almost fixed equilibrium so long existing there.

If a section, of say, fifty miles, in the richest portion of the Platte valley in Nebraska be carved

STATION ON THE OPEN STEPPES OF SIBERIA, ON THE TRANS-SIBERIAN RAILWAY, OVER ONE THOUSAND MILES EAST OF THE URAL MOUNTAINS AND ABOUT TWO THOUSAND TWO HUNDRED MILES EAST OF MOSCOW

out as a sample, there would be a strict resemblance between this and the country on the line of the Siberian railway, through the whole distance from the Ural Mountains to the Yenisei River, nearly 1,800 miles. Throughout this great distance, excepting a portion between the Obi and Yenisei, there is no timber save a species of small birch closely resembling the cottonwood of the Missouri

ON THE SIBERIAN STEPPES OR PRAIRIES, OVER ONE THOUSAND MILES EAST OF THE URAL MOUNTAINS, AND ABOUT TWO THOUSAND TWO HUNDRED MILES EAST OF MOSCOW

valley. Being scattered at wide intervals in small clumps throughout this vast country, it greatly heightens the similarity.

I have already said the line is almost level and straight as an arrow from the Obi to the Ural Mountains. I do not believe, for that space, the

ON THE SIBERIAN STEPPES, BETWEEN THE ISHIM AND IRTISH RIVERS, ON THE LINE OF THE SIBERIAN RAILWAY

line varied 300 feet from a true level. Along the whole line there is the most luxuriant growth of grass I have seen in any country. There are many varieties—some like the native blue stem of the West, and one variety that in appearance seemed closely allied to the Kentucky blue grass. Judging from the superb condition of the animals that graze upon them, they must all be of the most

RECENT SETTLEMENT ON SIBERIAN RAILWAY, BETWEEN THE OBI AND TOM RIVERS, ABOUT TWO THOUSAND FOUR HUNDRED MILES EAST OF MOSCOW

nutritious nature; it is, therefore, not only one of the finest, but by far the largest grazing regions in the world. If fully utilized, I believe Siberia could furnish the beef supply for the world. The soil seems similar to that of Eastern Nebraska and Kansas; in fact it is, in great part, identical with the Tschernozium formation in European Russia, an eastward extension of which it seems to be.

LAKE ON THE SIBERIAN STEPPES

The country for 600 miles was literally dotted with beautiful lakes of clear, pure water of one-half to two miles in diameter, the habitat, in the season, of myriads of ducks, geese, and other wild fowl. These lakes, as also the rivers, abound in fish of good quality and many varieties. The country is,

EMIGRANTS ON SIBERIAN STEPPES, EAST OF THE OBI RIVER

therefore, well watered and well drained. I saw scarcely any traces of alkali in the soil. There are many grouse and partridge in the steppes, but no deer of any kind; accountable, no doubt, to the

CHAPEL IN RECENTLY SETTLED TOWN ON SIBERIAN RAILWAY

long occupancy of the country by the Tartars, who convert it into a sort of semi-domestic domain.

As the railway management have for the moment made a liberal allotment of time in which the occasional passenger trains are to make the trip, frequent stops are made. At some of the larger towns the delay may be from two to five hours. I have availed myself of the opportunity thus given to acquire a knowledge of the country at some distance from the line, by jumping into a drosky and driving straight away from the road. At the breakneck speed they habitually drive, I have been enabled frequently to cover a distance from ten to twenty miles from the station.

After passing the Obi River the land, as far as the Yenisei, becomes more rolling and has a thicker growth of trees, the fir being present to some extent, with the birch. This region is almost exactly like Eastern Nebraska and the State of Iowa—the same rolling lands and deep, black soil. If possible, this is even better wheat land than the more level lands west of the Obi. From the Yenisei for about 600 miles, I am told that much the same country exists, until the mountain range near Lake Baikal is reached, running as a spur from the Altais in Northern China.

VII

Kurgan on the Tobol River—The Kirghiz Tartars—Their tents, villages, mode of life, etc.—The future of Kurgan—Winters in Siberia—No blizzards in Western Siberia—Rainfall—Petropavlovsk on the Ishim River—Rapid change in country on railway line—Emigrant trains eastward—Growth of grains on the line of railway—Surplus awaiting shipment—Omsk on the Irtish and Om rivers—Interesting character—Tomsk on the Tom River—The prison in Tomsk—Flourishing college—Electric lights, telephone system, and other conveniences—Condition of railroad east of Tomsk—Various excursions from Tomsk into the country.

The first town of importance after leaving Tscheljabinsk is Kurgan, once the seat of the Tartar government before its conquest by the Muscovite. It is situated on the Tobol River, which, after flowing 500 miles north, joins the Irtish at Tobolsk. Kurgan lies in the midst of what, in virtue of its extent, richness of soil, and exuberant pasturage, is perhaps the largest and best tract of grazing land on the globe. The town owes its importance to the large cattle trade that centres here from the Kirghiz steppes in all directions. It was a town of no inconsiderable importance before the railroad was constructed.

Here one sees the Kirghiz in his natural state, but little modified by modern civilization. They are a splendid race, having strong features and a dignified bearing, and are accredited with many virtues. It is said they are unusually cleanly

STATION AT KURGAN, SIBERIAN RAILWAY

and of notable fidelity and hospitality, especially where strangers are concerned. Being a purely pastoral people, they disdain the tillage of the soil, living almost wholly on the production of their herds. The life of the Tartar is a simple and monotonous one, and withal frugal. Their diet consists almost wholly of meats and cheese.

KIRGHIZ TARTAR, CAMELS, AND CAMEL CART. THESE CARTS ARE IN EXTENSIVE USE ON THE SIBERIAN STEPPES, CONSTITUTING, IN SEVERAL PLACES, THE CHIEF METHOD OF TRANSPORTATION

They have a peculiar drink called ayran, made of boiled milk diluted with water, and then allowed to stand until it slightly ferments and turns sour. It forms an excellent and most refreshing summer drink. Their various products

KIRGHIZ YURT OR TENT AND GROUP OF TARTARS ON THE SIBERIAN STEPPES, BETWEEN KURGAN AND PETROPAVLOVSK

of the dairy are kept in goat-skins. Their clothing and bedding they make themselves, and mostly from the felt and wool of the sheep and goat. The curious tents in which these people live, called yurts, and that are scattered in villages —called in Tartar, aul—throughout the wide steppes, are well known. They are made of a coarse felt, fully an inch thick, composed of the coarser varieties of sheep and goat's wool. The tents are round, with a dome-shaped cover, in the apex of which is a small aperture through which the smoke escapes from the fire built on the ground in the centre of the tent.

It is impossible, from the want of reliable statistics, to determine with any degree of accuracy the number of these people, who once swarmed in such multitudes, necessitating those periodic overflows the mere menace of which terrified even remote nations. But as they are scattered throughout an area of beautiful and fertile country two-thirds as large as the United States, they must yet number many hundreds of thousands. Their herds are mainly composed of cattle and sheep, although they have many fine horses and an occasional flock of goats. The quality of meat grown on these steppes is unsurpassed, I might almost say unequalled, as nothing can exceed the quality of the beef, mutton, and veal that are served at the railway stations on the line running through this region.

Kurgan is certainly cast for a large city, when once the great country tributary to it is utilized to anything like its full capabilities. Although you see everywhere immense herds of animals, and

TARTAR CAMEL TRAIN ON SIBERIAN STEPPES

although the country is checkered with newly ploughed fields, still it is apparent that its ultimate grazing and cereal resources have as yet been scarcely more than tested.

CHURCH IN NEW SIBERIAN VILLAGE

Although the winters are very cold, they are not especially long or trying. While the extreme temperature during winter may reach a point ten to fifteen degrees lower than in Ohio, or generally in latitude forty in the United States, still, as the air is very dry and there are no high winds. I have no doubt the winter season can be passed without especial discomfort. When winter sets in, which it does suddenly, and usually about the first of November, it continues steadily through about five months, when there is as sudden a breakup, ushering in permanently pleasant warm weather.

There are no mid-winter thaws, as in the United States, with their extremes of summer heat and polar chills, but the weather remains continuously cold, and the snow lies unbroken on the ground until the spring thaw. Nor is the snowfall excessive. By those who have the experience, I am informed that the winters are far more agreeable than in other countries, where the temperature is higher and more violent changes occur.

There is one climatic feature here that gives this country a marked advantage over our own great West, where a higher temperature prevails, and that is the entire absence of those blizzards which are the terror of our Western stockmen. I cannot remember having seen on the entire line of the Siberian railway more than one or two places where barriers were provided to protect the track from drifting snow. I am, indeed, told that the Tartars give their herds neither food nor protection in the winter, leaving them to take care of themselves,

A TARTAR PEASANT ON ROAD SOUTH OF OMSK.

which it is said they readily do by scratching away the snow that covers the tall, thick growth of grass beneath. The rainfall in summer is seasonable

ON THE POST-ROUTE FROM PETROPAVLOVSK TO OMSK

and abundant. I have been unable to make out to my own satisfaction where the rain comes from.

As in America, it invariably rains here when the rain-bearing clouds come from the south and west, and clears away with a north or northwest wind.

It is easy to understand why, in America, a south wind brings rain. As the current of air saturated with moisture from the Gulf and warm equatorial waters in the south comes in contact with the colder air of higher latitudes, it naturally deposits it in the form of rain. But as a south wind here comes from the high, cold plateau region of Central Asia, where the air is dry and evaporation meagre, it is not easy to see why a southern current of air under these conditions should deposit rain.

Petropavlovsk is the next town of importance reached. It is on the Ishim River, a tributary of the Obi, and it contains about 20,000 inhabitants. It was once the frontier fortress used by Russia against the Kirghiz. It owes its existence to an important trade with Samarkand and Central Asia, great trains of camels coming from those places. Like all the old towns on this route, new buildings and other evidences of rapid development attest the vivifying influence of the railroad.

From Petropavlovsk to Omsk, a distance of about 400 miles, there is the same monotonous repetition of level, fertile plains, flowery fields, budding villages, and newly cultivated lands. It is evident that the Russian policy of settling this country, which I will give you later on, is producing marked changes, especially in those parts rendered accessible by the railroad. For miles on

STATION AT PETROPAVLOVSK, SIBERIAN RAILWAY. GROUP OF KIRGHIZ TARTARS

each side of the line, as far as the Yenisei River, the lands are being taken, and in many places heavy crops are being raised. Long trains crowded with emigrants on their way eastward are frequently

STREET SCENE IN OMSK

passed. Of wheat and oats they have already produced a large surplus. All along the route, as far as Tomsk, one will see at the stations great piles of sacks containing wheat of last year's crop, which, on account of the congested traffic of the road, is awaiting shipment. This surplus is happily most opportune, as it will be shipped to the drought-stricken region 1,500 miles to the west, where, on account of excessive dry weather, in the fairest portion of Russia in the Volga valley, 300 miles wide and nearly 500 miles long, the crops have been almost an absolute failure and much distress exists.

Omsk, on the Irtish River, the second city of Siberia, with a population of 40,000, owes much of its importance to the fact that it is the capital of Western Siberia, which was moved from Tobolsk in 1824. Like all Siberian towns of this class, it has some elegant and even massive government buildings, along with many fine brick and stone business structures, all embedded in a mass of curiously built wooden houses. The streets, except the long one on which the business houses are located, and forming the artery of the town, are unpaved; much of the year they are almost impassable. Like all Russian towns, there are many fine churches in Omsk, some of them of great size, and, being always of the Oriental type of architecture, sometimes present an indescribably charming appearance.

At Omsk a most interesting character came aboard the train, on his way to Tomsk, returning thence to Moscow to attend the dedication there

EMIGRANTS AT STATION, BETWEEN PETROPAVLOVSK AND OMSK, ON SIBERIAN RAILWAY

of the monument to the Czar Alexander II., which is soon to take place and promises to be an imposing affair. He was a fine specimen of this hardy race, about sixty-five years of age, most intelligent and well educated. He is the mayor of quite an

STREET SCENE IN TOMSK

important city called Vernoe, in Southern Siberia in the Altai Mountains, over 1,000 miles southeast of Omsk. He had just driven from that city in a troika, a distance of 1,200 miles, in eight days. Having spent most of his life in that region, he had never before seen a railway. It was interesting to note his dazed and half-frightened appearance as the train moved off. Through my guide, I obtained from him much valuable information as

ON THE STEPPES OF SIBERIA, EAST OF KURGAN

to the nature of the great region lying south of the railway line.

He informed me that for 600 miles the same level, rich, black prairie lands extended. After that, by a gradual ascent through 500 or 600 miles further, the lands meanwhile growing more rolling and rougher, the summit of the Altais is reached at an elevation of 12,000 feet. All the cereals

DISTANT VIEW OF TOMSK

GROWTH OF CEREALS IN SIBERIA

grow there in great luxuriance and abundance. Even Indian corn throughout a great extent of that country grows and matures in the most perfect manner. The usual crop of wheat, he stated, was about thirty bushels per acre, and that of oats

MARKET SCENE IN TOMSK

about sixty bushels. The country, as a whole, is practically unsettled, being occupied mainly by a few roving tribes of Kalmuck or Kirghiz Tartars.

Tomsk is, perhaps, the most important and largest town in Siberia, and has had a rapid growth since the railway has been completed there. It is not on the main line, but eighty miles away on a branch running northward down the Tom Valley, and which in due time will be extended. It much resembles Omsk, having some fine government and business buildings. The prison is a huge, ugly, brick building, with low, vaulted corridors in the

VILLAGE IN SIBERIA, IN THE TOM RIVER VALLEY, ON THE POST-ROUTE FROM TOMSK TO TOBOLSK

interior, the whole of such gloomy aspect as to fully satisfy the most dismal imaginings of those who are disposed to believe in the horrors of Siberian prison life. There is a flourishing university in Tomsk, with 300 students and thirty professors. I might add that Tomsk is lighted by electric light and has a telephone system.

EMIGRANT TRAIN BETWEEN PETROPAVLOVSK AND OMSK, TWO THOUSAND MILES EAST OF MOSCOW

As the departure of trains eastward from Tomsk is most irregular and uncertain, being usually at intervals of from three to five days, this delay gave me an opportunity to make several interesting and

VIEW ON POST-ROUTE BETWEEN TOMSK AND IRKUTSK

instructive excursions far into the country, on the old post-routes running to Tobolsk and Irkutsk. In these I saw the native Russian life in its most provincial form. While there are a few good roads leading from Tomsk, there are many very bad ones.

VIII

Travelling on post and common roads in Russia and Siberia—Unique outfit—Splendor of private equipages—A Siberian tarantass—Manner of hitching the horses—Speed discomforts and excitement of travel on tarantass—Seeing Tartar life in its simplicity—A queer-looking vehicle—Homely but effective—Experience versus philosophy—Furious driving—The village sheik—A compatriot of the great Circassian Schemyl—A Mohammedan—His family life—Beauty and filial devotion of his children—His wives—Influence of the wife among the Kalmucks—Kirghiz village—Hospitality of our host—Our Yamstchik—His style and skill as a driver—Great speed of horses without use of whip—Return to Tomsk—Various modes of travel.

I HAD occasion before to refer to the manner in which travel is effected on the common roads of Russia. It is the same here, only they use vehicles more unique, and in some cases decidedly indigenous. As in European Russia, they invariably drive their horses abreast. In the droshkies about the cities, they generally use for common purposes one or two horses only; but in occasional turnouts, where display is the fad of the owner, a troika with three horses is used. Travelling through the country is done with three to seven horses,

TAIYORKA, A FIVE-HORSE TEAM ON SIBERIAN STEPPES

according to the condition of the road and the number of passengers to be carried; for it must be understood that the driver makes the same time and speed over rough and muddy roads as over smooth ones, having not the slightest regard for

ANOTHER MODE OF TRAVELLING IN SIBERIA.

either the safety or comfort of the luckless occupant. Nothing can surpass the *chic* of a first-class and well-appointed Russian or Siberian team when in full motion. The horses are all well kept and high spirited. The centre horse is hitched between shafts to guide the vehicle, and is usually the steadiest and most vigorous of the lot. For the outer horses, they generally select very handsome and alert ones, with long, flowing manes and tails carefully dressed. By some peculiar method of reining these horses, their heads are drawn low

STREET SCENE IN TOMSK

down and outward, causing them to pull at an angle from those in the middle. The cunning way in which they toss their pretty little heads and their other coquettish capers as they plunge along

SIBERIAN TARANTASS

at a full gallop, being in such marked contrast with the more sturdy and uniform gait of the central horses, impart an indescribable style and dash to the outfit.

Being desirous of seeing Tartar life in its simplest and primitive form, untouched by the ways of the city, I concluded to drive to a somewhat noted village to the southwest of Tomsk, where the camel trains from Samarkand to Irkutsk via Semipalatinsk cross those from the China border going northwest to Petropavlovsk. Being limited in time, as I desired to take the first train eastward, that was announced to leave in a few days, I instructed my guide to procure me a comfortable and suitable outfit for the expedition, and to arrange for our departure at an early hour. Having had a recent rain, and the roads therefore being somewhat heavy, he advised the use of a tarantass, with five horses, for a portion of the way, until the lighter roads on the higher lands were reached, when the journey could be completed with three horses.

On driving up in the morning, I took a swift glance at the strange-looking vehicle, and my guide looked at me with a suspicious smile. I had previously seen and travelled in the strange enough looking droshkies and troikas, but the sudden apparition of this nondescript took me completely aback. I said to my guide: "I know you speak English well enough, but I doubt your Russian, as this driver has evidently misunderstood your order, for instead of a tarantass, he has

NATIVE WAITING FOR FERRY ON TOM RIVER

brought me a specimen from some museum of natural history, as it looks more like a fossil skeleton of the paleozoic age, mounted on wheels, than a vehicle to make a long and tedious journey in." It looked as if the owner had built it in his back yard, with an inch auger and a hatchet. With many lively gestures, and, I suppose, choice and vigorous Tartar, he informed my guide that it was a real tarantass, a true Siberian tarantass, in fact, the best and most comfortable in the whole city,

CROSSING TOM RIVER, SIBERIA, ON A RUDE FERRY-BOAT

and that it was perfectly safe. I despair of worthily describing this strange assemblage of parts, the intricate network of poles, braces, and ribs, all lashed and bound together with leather thongs, and not a nail or bolt in it. Excepting the linch-pin and the tires on the wheels, I don't believe there was an ounce of iron in its whole composition. It seemed to me it was in imminent danger of rattling to pieces like a child's toy house.

It was wholly without springs, and to break the shock due to inequalities of the road, reliance was placed entirely on the pliability of the structure and the elasticity of the almost rigid poles upon which the body was mounted. To a rather contemptuous look, born of a remembrance of our own mighty achievements in iron and steel in the West, he replied that the vehicle was well constructed, and that it was all right, and, indeed, to perform the services required of it it could be made in no other way. Alas, for the previsions of human wisdom! The event proved that he was correct, and furnished additional evidence that the crude results of a blind and awkward experience often upset the refined deductions of a speculative philosophy. After being thumped and bumped about for twenty-four hours, I came to have more respect for the skill that put the parts together so as to safely yield to the irregularities of the road, which must certainly prove fatal to one rigidly constructed.

In fact, this was illustrated a few days later in an uncomfortable manner when, taking another tarantass of a new pattern, equipped with steel axles, we had not driven a mile before one of the axles snapped short off near the wheel, bringing us down in one common ruin, and we were obliged to complete our journey in the old reliable one. The

AT THE POST-HOUSE

body of our vehicle was a sort of shallow basket and without seats. It was filled with hay, on which you sit in the bottom in a half-reclining position. I had no sooner nestled myself down in the hay than the driver leaped into his seat and the horses suddenly dashed into such a furious pace as to well-nigh jerk me out of the vehicle and wrench my spine from my body.

The rain of the previous night had caused the road to be cut into many deep ruts and into what we call in the West "chuck holes." I soon discovered that the injunction to my guide to make good time was being only too literally followed by the driver. Off he flew at a full gallop, the horses going literally *ventre à terre*, just as if he were driving over the finest roads of France. All protests were unavailing, for I afterwards learned that before starting he had stoutly recruited himself from his bottle of vodka, which stuck conspicuously out of his pocket. I also felt somewhat reassured when my guide told me that it was quite the custom in this country to drive in this manner on a long trip, when good time was required. On reaching the first village where relays were to be provided, I found that we had covered a distance of nearly twenty versts—almost fourteen miles—in a trifle over an hour.

After refreshing ourselves with a cup of tea from the ubiquitous samovar, which you find everywhere, we resumed our journey. On the roads becoming smoother, we reduced our team to three horses, and without any abatement of our

TAKING TEA "AL FRESCO" WITH A RUSSIAN FAMILY AT POST-HOUSE

pace we finally reached our destination, where I alighted to take an inventory of my damaged anatomy. There was no means of knowing the

RUSSIAN VILLAGE ON POST-ROUTE, SOUTH OF TOMSK, SIBERIA

distance, of course, but, judging from my feelings, I should think it was a thousand miles, more or less.

On arrival, as is the custom of these people, the sheik of the village took charge of us. Being the important personage here, his house was of pretentious proportions and constructed of hewed logs much after the Russian custom, forming a large square which enclosed a rectangular space. He was evidently a man not only of much influ-

READY TO START. AT THE POST-HOUSE, ON POST-ROUTE SOUTH OF TOMSK, IN DIRECTION TOWARD SEMIPALATINSK.

ence, but also of great wealth, for he pointed with pride to his great herds of horses, cattle, and sheep on the adjacent plains. He informed us that he was a compatriot of Schemyl, and fought with that celebrated chieftain against the Musco-

CATHEDRAL IN TOMSK

vite. He also exhibited with much pride a medal given him by the present Czar when as Crown Prince he visited this region, and whose guide he was. He at once extended those little courtesies

STREET SCENE IN TOMSK

and substantial comforts that have made these people so famous for their hospitality.

I had no sooner entered his apartments than I discovered, by the familiar appointments of his household, that he was a Mohammedan. He at once, as is the manner of these people, brought in and introduced his children, of whom he was intensely fond, an affection fully reciprocated by them, a characteristic which I long since observed is true of all Asiatics. He had two most lovely little boys of ten to twelve years of age, and a daughter of surpassing beauty.

As he himself and his favorite wife—for he had several—were of Caucasian descent, she reflected in the highest degree the exquisite beauty for which her race is noted. The inimitable purity of her complexion; the soft, dreamy eyes of the Circassian; her delightful naïveté of manner, combined with an exquisite Oriental costume, made her a veritable Lalla Rookh. In a short time the mother appeared, a stately, matronly lady; for, although having three or four wives, like so many Mohammedans, he has one who is the wife who shares with him the duties and honors of the household.

After drinking the tea and eating the sweetmeats they invariably offer, I requested my guide to say to him that, being from the far-off land of America, I would be pleased to be permitted to take a photograph of his family, as I had a camera with me. Knowing that it is against the tenets of the Koran to in any way reproduce in picture

KIRGHIZ TARTAR FAMILY ON SIBERIAN STEPPES. THE TARTAR YURT OR TENT

the human form, I was doubtful of his consenting to so extraordinary a proceeding. After a long hesitation, he requested that he might consult his wife.

It is surprising what an influence the wife possesses in this polygamous country. I am told that among the Kalmuck Tartars the husband will not sell even a sheep without first consulting her. He finally replied that the Koran did indeed forbid the making of pictures of themselves, but it did not say that an American could not photograph them. Gladly accepting the soundness of this subtle distinction, I had my guide quickly photograph the group.

The village, like all true Kirghiz villages, is composed of a cluster of the round felt tents or yurts I have already referred to. A beautiful little mosque, built of something like adobe, rises conspicuously from the assemblage of tents. They tend their flocks on the distant steppes, and are superb horsemen. Before the building of the railway, which has given them a nearer market, their traffic was conducted at Samarkand in the south and Kurgan in the northwest.

After taking many views of caravans, costumes, tents, etc., we prepared for our return. As is the custom, there was preliminary to this an exchange of small presents with the host and his family

He wanted particularly to know my address in Moscow, as he desired to send me there, in the form of some substantial present, a token of his regards. We left carrying with us a most agreeable impression of the rude but sincere hospitality of these people.

Our driver was a full Kalmuck. As his race, unlike the Kirghiz, devote their attention almost wholly to the rearing of horses, they are therefore experts in all that appertains to that noble animal. It was truly wonderful the way he handled his unwieldly team. The trappings of his harness were like the rigging of a ship. I marveled how he managed when driving at such a great speed that they did not become a hopeless tangle. As he never used a whip, making with his mouth simply an occasional buzzing sound, I am still wondering how he so silently and quietly urged his horses into such a furious gait, which they seldom broke. His posture when driving at full speed, the ease and grace with which he controlled the reins in his well-filled hands, gave a style that might well be the despair of any fashionable whip of London or New York. I have traveled in California stages, Japanese jinrikshas, Arabian caravans, and Hindoo ox-garries, but I must say that a Siberian tarantass, engineered by a Kalmuck Yamstchik with a little vodka for fuel, easily beats the record.

GREAT FORTY-TON BELL AT CATHEDRAL IN TOMSK

At the distance of two or three miles from Tomsk there is a splendid race-course, at which excellent meetings are often held. Being the season when the great annual event was to occur, I visited the course, that I might study the sporting

ON THE TURF AT TOMSK

side of life in this remote region. Along the whole route I was surprised to see the road literally crowded with superb equipages, filled with ladies and gentlemen evidently of the very best class. Many of the ladies were exquisitely costumed, obviously in what was the very latest product of Parisian art. The roadside was well lined with pedestrians wending their way to the races. In fact, were it not for strong local peculiarities and coloring, that reminded one that he was in a far-off inter-Asiatic city, one might easily imagine that he was on the road to the Saratoga races, or to Epsom Downs. Here, as in almost every place in Russian possessions, we were constantly surprised to find how closely the people of this great empire follow the customs and progress, and adopt the conveniences and improvements, of other countries. The vehicles used on the course I found, to my astonishment, were of the very latest and best patterns to be found in the most progressive and up-to-date countries. I found in Omsk, Tomsk, and other Siberian towns that rubber tires were in such general use as to attract no attention. In fact, I believe that in Moscow and St. Petersburg this useful and almost novel device is in more general use than in either Paris, London, or New York. The races here were mainly running and trotting. I was especially interested in a running race where little Tartar boys were the riders. They rode bare-backed, and coming of a race who almost live on horseback, the skill and agility they very naturally displayed was at once surprising and amusing. The crowd at the races, being of the usual mixed character, was,

ON THE HOME STRETCH

however, excellent in its deportment. In truth, I have never seen a more quiet, peaceful, and orderly assemblage of people on any public oc-

STREET SCENE IN TOMSK

casion. What surprised me greatly was the almost entire absence of either betting or intoxication, as I was somehow led into the belief that the Russians were great gamblers as well as drinkers, and expected to find here striking exhibitions of both.

Krasnoyarsk is on the Yenisei River and is practically now the end of the Siberian railway, at least so far as passenger traffic is concerned. Tomsk is the terminus of the present through passenger service, from which place, however, an ordinary train is run about once a week to the Yenisei River. Although the track is laid for nearly 600 miles further eastward to Lake Baikal and near Irkutsk, only an occasional mixed freight and passenger train is put on this section; but no one can tell when it is to depart — a fact only made known by the officials three or four days in advance. Travel, therefore, from here eastward becomes most uncertain as well as very uncomfortable.

There is no bridge over the Yenisei, the crossing at present being done on a rather rude and imperfect ferry. They are busily engaged in the construction of a handsome iron bridge nearly a mile in length. It will be completed in a few months, when it will be possible to make a continuous journey on a fairly comfortable through train to Irkutsk and Lake Baikal, a distance of nearly 4,000 miles east of Moscow.

The gold mines here and in the hills beyond furnish some measure of varied interest to the

WASHERWOMEN AT TOMSK

weary and expectant traveller. They are mainly placer mines, but in the foot-hills of the Altai Mountains, which the road approaches near Irkutsk, quartz mining is being developed. The mining

RAILWAY STATION ON SIBERIAN RAILWAY, BETWEEN THE OBI ANDTOM RIVERS, ABOUT ONE THOUSAND ONE HUNDRED MILES EAST OF THE URAL MOUNTAINS

interests generally are said to be rapidly growing, with much promise for the future. Being largely the property of the government, but few details concerning them can be obtained as to their future possibilities, as they are shrouded with the usual official secrecy of this country.

As I have now travelled about 3,000 miles in Siberia by railway, troika, tarantass, and otherwise, I am debating in my mind whether I shall proceed farther eastward, or begin my return from this region. It is possible to go some hundreds of miles farther on by rail, but it is doubtful if what one sees will be an adequate reward for the delays and hardships encountered. I am told that, for the most part, the country and scenery are quite the same as I have been looking at for weeks—the same succession of fertile plains, with their wondrous growth of grass, bedecked at times by a sea of flowers, and stretching far away to the horizon like a billowy ocean; the same crowds of emigrants in streams and train-loads to the country beyond, and the same embryo towns springing up everywhere like mushrooms from the earth; all of which, however surprising and interesting it may be in the outstart, becomes at last a wearisome monotony.

Another consideration influences my return without going farther eastward. I desire to consume several days in an examination of the larger towns on the route, which I had not the opportunity of doing on my way hither. It is, moreover, my intention to leave the railway at Kurgan, and cut across the country to the Caspian Sea by the route followed by the camel trains between those points.

STATION ON THE TRANS-SIBERIAN RAILWAY, BETWEEN TOMSK AND TAIGA

It follows the Tobol River a hundred miles or so, and then crosses the Kirghiz steppes, finally reaching the Caspian Sea, where the ships leave for Baku. The distance is about 800 miles, and as the roads are said to be fairly good, the journey can be comfortably made in a little over a week. Crossing the Caspian Sea, I will go through the Caucasus, said to be the loveliest mountain scenery in the world; then via Tiflis to Batoum; from thence to Rostoff on the Don, and to Moscow and St. Petersburg. I will then have completed, in so far as is practicable, a tour of a large part of what is destined to become the mightiest empire on the globe.

IX

Return westward—Route across the Kirghiz steppes to the Caspian Sea—Down the Volga River to Astrakhan—Rise and commercial importance of that city—Modern trade diversion and its effects—Russia a land of fairs—Nijni Novgorod and its great fair—Kharkov, Iinsk, and other leading fairs—Preferred route across the Caspian Sea to Central Asia—Importance of the Volga River as a means of transportation—Numerous fleets of coal-oil barges—Statistics of freight traffic on the Volga and Onega system—Partiality of Russians for American products and methods.

ASTRAKHAN, *September*, 1898.

RETURNING westward, I found on inquiry at Kurgan that the route I had intended taking from that town to the Caucusus via the Caspian Sea, while easily accomplished in eight days, was likely to prove devoid of interest, unless one is supposed never to tire of what is wholly rural and pastoral.

There are no cities of importance on the entire route, only a few Russian villages settled by recent immigrants into that region from the older and congested districts of European Russia, numerous Tartar auls, and an occasional caravansary for the accommodation of the many camel trains that travel over this route, of which I have seen here

STREET SCENE IN ASTRAKHAN

and in other quarters of the globe more than enough.

I, therefore, came westward to the point where the Siberian railway first touches the Volga River at

ON THE VOLGA RIVER

Samara. From that town I came on one of the multitude of splendid passenger steamers that ply this mighty river — the Mississippi of Russia — to Astrakhan at the head of the Caspian Sea, a distance of over 1,000 miles.

This is a fine old city that justly ranks as a very ancient one, dating in its origin close back to the Christian era. It has a population of about 150,000, of such complex nature as might be expected at a point where the commercial advantages belong-

FIRE WORSHIPPERS' TEMPLE IN ASTRAKHAN

ing to it have caused the mixed people of Asia to converge through centuries for the purposes of trade.

It has many well-paved streets, and handsome public and business buildings. One of the churches most noted in all Russia for its imposing and ex-

THE KREMLIN IN ASTRAKHAN

pensive interior decorations is here. The city is well supplied with street railways, water-works, etc., and the glare of the electric light indicates

SCENE ON THE LANDING AT ASTRAKHAN

that it is well provided with many of the up-to-date luxuries and accessories of other more progressive and pretentious cities. It owes its origin and importance to the fact that for centuries it was the main point of commercial contact between the merchants of Central Asia and those of the western world, being, in fact, the entrepôt where Oriental products were concentrated for Western distribution. The Caspian Sea, on the one hand, furnished for Central Asia a means for transporting its products to the mouth of the Volga, whence on that river and its tributaries they found their way northward and westward to the European markets.

As before the days of steamships and railways Astrakhan had practically a monopoly of Central Asian traffic, she continued to grow and prosper until the development of railways in Russia and a more perfect system of river and canal transportation made Nijni Novgorod her great competitor as a grand distributing point of eastern and western products, which, through her wonderful annual markets, she held for many years.

Such, however, is the rapidity with which trade and its methods change in these modern days, that Nijni in turn has lost much of its importance, and at no distant day will cease largely to occupy its present position as an intermediate depot between Asia and Europe, an advantage that gave first to Astrakhan, and afterwards to Nijni, such commercial prominence and wondrous growth. Such are the ample and ever-increasing facilities for trade now supplied by railways, steamships, telegraphs, etc., that the merchants of the extreme East and West can now rapidly and directly communicate,

VIEW OF THE UPPER TOWN OF NIJNI NOVGOROD, ON NORTH BANK OF THE VOLGA

or easily meet, in the marts of their respective countries, so that an intermediate trading point or centre is fast becoming wholly unnecessary.

Russia is essentially a land of fairs, there being held in the various villages, towns, and cities throughout the empire nearly 3,000 every year, at which over 300,000,000 dollars' worth of goods and merchandize is sold. Of these, Nijni Novgorod, two hundred miles east of Moscow, at the junction of the Okra and Volga rivers, stands first in rank; and, indeed, with very few exceptions, the world has never seen anything more extensive and important than the annual fairs held in this city since 1817. At Irbit, in the government of Perm, in the Ural Mountains, there is also held an annual fair of much importance, at which the sales amount to over 30,000,000 dollars annually.

With the fairs at Kharkov, Ilinsk, Romny, and a few others, a list would be completed of those of the leading class or first magnitude. Of the second class there are fifty; there are sixty of the third, and over 500 of the fourth class. The balance, of nearly 2,500, are those held in the towns, villages, and communes. The Nijni Novgorod fair is officially in operation scarcely five weeks, in the months of July and August. The important position it holds in the internal trade of Russia will be realized from the fact that in this short time nearly 100,000,000 dollars' worth of wares and merchandise is sold.

It is my present intention to go from here via

TOWN ON THE VOLGA RIVER BETWEEN KAZAN AND NIJNI NOVGOROD

the Caspian Sea to Baku, a distance of 600 miles. From there, crossing the Caspian Sea to Uzum Ada, I am in hopes of getting a permit to go on the military railway that runs through the trans-Caspian region to Merv, Bokhara, Samarkand,

VIEW OF NIJNI NOVGOROD, WHERE THE GREAT FAIR IS HELD, ON SOUTH SIDE OF THE VOLGA

and Tashkent, right into the very heart of Asia—
a trip that is rarely made, and until recent years
a region almost inaccessible to people of the West.
Samarkand, especially on account of its antiquities
and its having been the capital of Tamerlane, I
desire very much to visit.

Returning to Baku, I will take one of the steamers that run hence daily to Lenkoran, in Northern Persia, through which I will return via Erivan, at the base of Mt. Ararat, which city is the present capital of Armenia. From there I will go to Tiflis, through Kars and Erzerum; then passing over the Caucasian Mountains to Vladikavkaz, I will take the railway there for Moscow, hoping to arrive in that city about the middle or end of November.

As, for the present at least, it is my intention to write only of my observations and experiences in Siberia, I must, therefore, forego the temptation to give in detail, and refer only briefly to, the objects of interests one sees on a voyage down the Volga. I may, however, say in passing that the trade and travel on this great highway are little short of wonderful. The large, comfortable passenger boats, of best pattern and most approved machinery, can be numbered almost by hundreds, and the steam, freight, and tugboats that swarm on this great river, almost by thousands.

These, with the numerous fleets of barges with coal oil from Baku, and other merchandise, give more the appearance of the Hudson between New

PICTURESQUE FORMATION ON THE VOLGA RIVER, TWO HUNDRED MILES ABOVE ASTRAKHAN

York and Yonkers, than of a river traversing the open steppes of Russia.

Statistics show that the waterways forming the Volga-Onega system carry yearly over 15,000,000 tons of freight. Of grain alone, this river and

THE CATHEDRAL IN NIJNI NOVGOROD

its tributaries carry over 100,000,000 bushels annually. Along with many evidences one meets everywhere in Russia of her partiality for and

WATERMELON MARKET AT LANDING ON THE VOLGA RIVER, BETWEEN SIMBIRSK AND SARATOV

admiration of things American, I would say that the boats used on the Volga are almost exclusively those of the American pattern.

Development of Siberian agricultural resources—Its effect upon similar interests in other countries—Prime conditions governing the future reclamation of lands in Siberia—Waterways of Russia—Careful development of same—River system in Siberia—Severity of winters restrict their use—Season of navigation—Omsk as a centre of a vast cereal region—Its possible connections by water and rail with foreign countries—Necessity for greater transportation facilities in Western Siberia—New route being created from Omsk to the Baltic—New route between Russia and Western Siberia—From Omsk to Havre or London—Comparative distances.

The general facts and data I have given respecting the possible agricultural resources of Siberia very naturally will suggest the pertinent inquiry as to what influence their ultimate development will have upon similar interests in other countries. To a nation like our own, where agriculture is the dominant industry, and upon the healthfulness of which depends almost all other industrial interests, and whose exportable surplus forms our most valuable national resource, this inquiry possesses exceptional interest and importance.

As the prime factor in this question is the rapidity with which these lands can be developed—

FISHING VILLAGE ON THE OBI RIVER, SIBERIA

this governing the possible exportable surplus—an inquiry into this subject will fall naturally under several heads, the chief being transportation facilities for internal and external purposes, the

TOWN ON THE LOWER VOLGA RIVER

policy of the government as to the settlement of the lands, and the relation of growth of population to any possible rate of agricultural development.

I have heretofore stated that the Russian government has under contemplation a somewhat extended system of railways for the whole of Siberia, both for strategical and commercial purposes. They, however, by no means rely wholly on railways for transportation.

VIEW ACROSS TOM RIVER, SIBERIA

Like all European countries, the utmost care is here taken for the preservation, development, and improvement of her natural and artificial waterways. She is, in addition to the most careful use of all her rivers, contemplating vast schemes of canal construction to supplement and interweave her river courses. As a result, not only the main stems, but even the smallest tributaries of her large rivers are made serviceable for the uses of transportation in the highest degree, so that internal distribution of tonnage is effected throughout the country by a very intricate network of navigable rivers and improved streamlets, often linked together by suitable canals.

So pronounced is the policy favoring water transportation here, that one never sees what has so often happened in our own country, and which is much to be deplored—the subordination of natural and artificial waterways to other methods of transportation, and even, in some cases, their total destruction.

As I have before pointed out, the whole of Siberia is traversed from south to north by large rivers, at intervals of a few hundred miles. These rivers invariably spread out fan-like into numerous branches, all of which are navigable, or can be rendered so, through much of their length and during a large portion of the year. To almost the southern boundary of Siberia, therefore, water transportation can ultimately be effected.

Vast as is this natural system of waterways, its efficiency will, of course, be somewhat curtailed by the severity of the winters in Northern Siberia. But under the wise fostering policy of the government, there will no doubt in time be rendered as efficient a system of rivers and canals as now exists in European Russia, and which plays so important a part in her internal commerce.

These rivers, it is said, are open for navigation

FERRY-BOAT ON TOM RIVER, SIBERIA

usually from about the middle of April or 1st of May to the 1st of October. This gives quite six months of continuous navigation, which is not greatly exceeded by our great chain of northern lakes, and canals such as the Erie, which, while open, have such an important bearing on rates and the freight traffic of the whole country.

As the Obi and Yenisei rivers with their tribu-

HOUSES FOR STORAGE OF GRAIN AND WHEAT IN SACKS AWAITING SHIPMENT AT NEW RAILWAY STATION, EIGHT HUNDRED MILES EAST OF THE URAL MOUNTAINS, ON TRANS-SIBERIAN RAILWAY

taries permeate the entire western half of Siberia, and the distance of Omsk, the centre of the great grain and pasture lands of that country, from European markets is about 5,000 miles via the Arctic

Sea, therefore for nearly six months an area of agricultural lands nearly equal in extent to the arable lands of the United States will be in almost

SCENE ON THE IRTISH RIVER, SIBERIA

as direct and continuous communication with Western Europe as is Chicago via the Great Lakes and St. Lawrence River.

The necessity of providing more adequate means for transporting the surplus agricultural products already created by the Siberian railway has fully impressed itself on the Russian mind. The present congested condition of that line, which is likely to grow worse, has caused the projection of several competing routes, to give this much-needed relief.

VIEW ACROSS THE IRTISH RIVER, SIBERIA.

A railway is already under construction running directly eastward from St. Petersburg to Perm, to connect with the railway now running from that city over the Ural Mountains to Tiumen, on the headwaters of the Tobol River.

This line will, therefore, provide direct communication between Omsk and the Baltic Sea, in competition with the Siberian line, which it will parallel 300 or 400 miles to the north. Indeed, for the season of river navigation this route is now practically available.

On my way eastward, I fell in with a prominent

VIEW ACROSS THE TOM RIVER, SIBERIA

Russian grain merchant, who was on his way to Omsk to establish a line of transportation to the Baltic, in order to drain some of the large surplus of grain already accumulated on the line of the Trans-Siberian railway, which for want of sufficient facilities it finds itself incapable of carrying. He described to me in detail the proposed new route, which was down the Irtish River from Omsk and up the Tobol to Tiumen, a distance of about 800 miles. From Tiumen, connection is to be made by rail to Perm on the Kama River, a distance of 500 miles.

At the latter point, boats run down the Kama River and up the Volga to the head of navigation of that river, where, by a canal to the Ladoga Sea and through the Neva, a continuous waterway is provided between Perm and the Baltic Sea. Thus, by this route, excepting the intermediate link of 500 miles of railroad, Omsk can be placed, via the Baltic, in direct communication by water with Western Europe for at least six months of the year, the whole distance being somewhat less than from Chicago to Liverpool or Havre.

XI

Transportation route in Southwestern Siberia—Route between Caspian and Black seas—To connect the Volga and Don rivers—All-waterway between Caspian Sea and Europe—Neglect of American waterways—Careful preservation of same in Europe—Methods of utilizing rivers in Europe for transportation purposes—Use of the Seine in France—Through the heart of France in a boat—Neglect and decay of American rivers as lines of transport—Railways versus water transportation—What would result from thorough development of American river system—Russia's real progress—Great foresight—Not doomed to the fate of China—Russia in the field of diplomacy—The official class—Redundant population—Its danger to all nations—Unwisdom of developing urban at the expense of the rural population—Results in the necessity for land grabbing—Wise policy underlying settlement of Siberia—Plan of settlement—Conserving old vested interests—Deterrent influences in settlement of Siberia—Rapid growth of population—Its current necessities—Probable effect of Siberia upon markets in other countries.

There are yet two other routes in prospect, which, when completed, will be both short and direct. By a system of railways in Southwestern Siberia, of 500 to 1,500 miles in length, reinforced by canal and river courses, a thorough drainage of tonnage to the east coast of the Caspian Sea can be effected from that vast region, being in extent equal to the Middle and Western States of

WHARF-BOAT AND LANDING ON VOLGA RIVER, BELOW TZARITZIN

our country, and with a productive capacity equal to one-half that of the whole United States. From the eastern shore of the Caspian Sea ships can be run at all seasons to Baku in the Caucasus.

By the Trans-Caucasian railway, a distance of a little less than 500 miles, the Caspian Sea is connected with the Black Sea. This will, therefore, make an open-water route the whole season from the Caspian to Western Europe, a distance of about 5,500 miles. Save the connecting link of railway from Baku to Batoum, a distance of about 500 miles, there will, therefore, be a continuous water route from Southwestern Siberia to Europe, from the east shore of the Caspian Sea.

The other scheme, while of the highest order, both from an engineering point of view and commercial as well, and while fully surveyed and estimated, is yet "under the red cloth," as the Russians say, meaning that it is still enveloped in the shrouded councils of "The Ministry of Transportation and Communication."

At Tzaritzin, about 300 miles above Astrakhan, the Volga River approaches within fifty miles of the Don River, running northward from the Black Sea. It is proposed to cut a canal across this intervening space to connect the two rivers, both of which will be navigable to this point three-fourths of the year. By this route, therefore, a continuous waterway can be established for nine months in the year between the Caspian Sea and the markets of Western Europe, via the Volga and Don rivers and the Black Sea.

When the water and railway systems of Western Siberia are perfected, as they will be in due time, that great country, with its vast and yet untouched agricultural resources, will be placed quite as near the surplus-consuming centres of Europe as the centre of the great surplus-producing region of the United States.

I desire at this point to make especial reference to what I have so frequently spoken of heretofore, viz.: the lamentable neglect of our splendid system of waterways, which stands in such startling contrast with the careful and thorough development and preservation of the natural and artificial water-courses in almost all other countries. To the observing American tourist, whose mind is at all bent upon a study of the material interests and resources of the countries through which he travels, nothing strikes him with such force—with the sole exception, perhaps, of the splendid common roads—as the careful and thorough manner in which every river or stream of any size is utilized for transportation purposes.

Everywhere one sees the river beds deepened by dredging, the channel widened, the banks carefully walled, and the shores suitably jettied, and every means employed to render them suitable for navigation. So thoroughly is this done, especially in France, Germany, Italy, Austria, and to a great extent in this country, that little bits of streams only a few rods wide are by suitable flash dams and other means converted into excellent channels for boats.

It is thus that in France the Seine is made navigable from the sea to Tonnerre, where it becomes an insignificant streamlet. From this point, over the Burgundy hills, a canal of about sixty miles forms a connecting link with the headwaters of the Rhone flowing southward. A boat, therefore, of considerable tonnage can pass right through the centre of France to the Mediterranean Sea.

By the same means, as I have before stated, a continuous waterway is provided through the middle of European Russia from the Baltic to the Caspian Sea.

It is with sorrow mingled with disgust that one recalls the shameless neglect of our mighty river systems, the grandest on the globe—the Mississippi, the Ohio, the Missouri, and scores of other rivers with their tributaries—and even the complete abandonment of the Wabash, the Illinois, and many others that in early days were so valuable and serviceable, and could still by a little attention be so maintained.

What can be said of the policy of a country that will allow such an important trade artery as the old Wabash and Erie Canal to become extinct? You and I well know that it was this valuable waterway, running from Terre Haute to Toledo, that developed and enriched the great Wabash valley, which remained one of the most prosperous and flourishing regions of the whole West until the withering touch of the overstocked and much manipulated Wabash Railway sapped and absorbed its accumulated resources.

With the noblest river on the globe permeating with its many tributaries almost the entire region from whence our exportable agricultural surplus has been derived, and will in future continue wholly to be derived, and which could be carried entirely by water to the consumptive centres of Europe, we to-day discover the astounding situation that our country is almost exclusively dependent upon the railways to carry this great surplus to the seaboard.

Were our main rivers only, to say nothing of the smaller streams that other countries would readily render serviceable, improved and utilized to anything like the degree of the Seine, Rhone,

Garonne, and Marne of France; the Elbe, Rhine, and other streams of Germany; the Danube, the Don, the Volga; and for that matter even the Obi of Siberia, no nation on the globe would possess such facilities for cheap transportation to foreign countries; so that no matter what natural advantages of agriculture they might possess in Siberia, Argentina, India, or elsewhere, we would be placed beyond competition in foreign markets.

When will those patriotic spirits who have the public ear, and who are ever on the alert to safeguard the public right and welfare, cry out against those influences and abnormal causes that have resulted in creating a situation so exceptional as to be well-nigh criminal?

Whatever may be the disparaging comparisons of the slower methods and material progress of Russia with the more florid achievements of other nations in recent years, it is certain that her progress is on such lasting, conservative, and secure lines that in the end, when viewed in its entirety, it may prove a more real advance than others more rapid and consequently less stable. Whatever may be her final and declared policy, she adheres to it with a steadfastness and pertinacity unchangeable and unconquerable.

Like China, she is preëminently an agricultural nation, that interest absorbing nearly four-fifths of her energies and nearly nine-tenths of her population. This great interest she fosters with the wisest foresight and the most jealous care.

Unlike her great neighbor, however, who had come to rely upon the virtues and power of peace, Russia has long foreseen that military strength alone could preserve a national autonomy against the forces of foreign aggression and greed, marshalled under the specious banner of philanthropy and progress. This fortunate foresight, no doubt, saves her from the fate of wholesale spoliation that now threatens China.

While Russia has the most numerous army in the world, and has created the largest national military element to draw from in case of emergency, still her policy is not to use her military power for conquest, but mainly for defence. Her great acquisitions of territory, amounting to one-seventh of the whole globe, have been acquired much more by diplomacy in the cabinet than by power in the field. Yet, as the stern and memorable records of Borodino and the bloody fields of the Crimea show, when called upon to defend her country, her skill and valor in the field are not inferior to her ability in the realm of diplomacy.

Never, perhaps, in the history of the human race has any nation acquired such vast possessions, or developed so large a population, equal to the Roman Empire in its palmiest days, with such little bloodshed and such few destructive wars.

The one great national characteristic of Russia seems to be foresight. She deals not so much with the present as the future, not with the proximate and immediate so much as with the remote and ultimate; and it seems to be a fixed policy never to commit herself to any scheme or plan unless the ultimate results are so well forecast as to render any retrogression or retracing of her steps unnecessary.

Moreover, there is perhaps no nation whose official classes are so well informed, or who so minutely understand the commercial, industrial, and even the political policies of other nations, and the real working and ultimate trend of their institutions. It was, no doubt, this penetrating foresight that caused her, long ago, to devise her policy of territorial acquisition, under which she laid aside for future use such vast, accessible, and contiguous areas of country which to the rest of the world seemed then useless.

The pressure of a redundant population always has been, and perhaps will remain, the chief peril threatening the stability of every nation. This danger becomes intensified when a nation by conquests, or ill-ordered fiscal policies, develops its commercial, manufacturing, and urban population at the expense of rural life.

In the cry, "Give us bread and amusement," that was current in Rome during the Cæsars, is to be found the germ of a force far more potent and fatal to that empire than the rapacity of the Hun or the military prowess of the Goth.

Even now, the same cause is impelling some of the foremost nations to resort to the doubtful expedient of forcing themselves upon peaceful, remote, and older nations, in the hope thereby of finding relief from pressing internal forces.

The acquisition of Siberia and Central Asia, a practically uninhabited and contiguous country, having over 7,000,000 square miles with less than 12,000,000 inhabitants, was, no doubt, the result of Russian foresight to secure near at home, and adjacent, a suitable reservoir into which to pour her future and increasing surplus population, providing thereby for centuries a safety valve for her empire. This lies at the very bottom of her settlement and development of Siberia and the Central Asian provinces, reserving them as she does for the steadily increasing future necessities of the older portions of her empire, rather than following the example of other nations, who, by a rapid development of new territory, quickened into an undue, intense, and transient life other subsidiary and dependent interests and industries.

From what I can learn, it will probably be the policy of Russia to make the settlement and development of Siberia commensurate with the necessities arising out of the rapid growth of population in the parent country, which, however, at its present rate, promises to be of no mean order.

In the first place, it is only citizens of Russia that can acquire lands in Siberia. A systematic plan is pursued by the government in the distribution and disposition of the lands. Wherever there is found an overpopulated district in European Russia, influences are at once used to cause an emigration of a portion of such congested district. Government agents are sent to Siberia to look about and secure for such emigrants the most suitable localities, due regard being had for racial peculiarities and proclivities, and even for the geographical locality of the intending emigrant. As an inducement, nearly eighty acres of land is alloted to each settler, and as a further stimulus the government in many cases loans 100 rubles for a term of years, without interest, to bona fide settlers upon the lands.

As I have before stated, Western Siberia lies practically between the same parallels of latitude as European Russia; the southern part touching a lower latitude, possesses, therefore, a more genial climate. The soil and physical characteristics are even more desirable, the only drawback being its greater distance from the market. Under these circumstances it is easy to see that a great flow of immigrants has already set into that country, as is evidenced on all hands by crowded trains, newly ploughed fields, and numerous embryo towns and villages.

Already the government is considering the important question as to what is to be the probable influence of the relatively cheaper products of these new lands, so readily acquired and so cheaply cultivated, upon the agricultural interests of the older portions of the empire, where lands have been longer cultivated and fixed investments are greater.

Being desirous of conserving the vested interests and rights of the agricultural classes in European Russia which have been the laborious creation of centuries, she does not lose sight of the injurious effect that may arise to them by the inflow of the products of these lands, the gift of the nation, the government thus becoming itself an indirect party to the sudden creation of an unjust and perhaps injurious competition.

As a measure designed to aid in overcoming such an effect, and to preserve a just equality, I was informed that the government contemplates giving rebates upon grain and other agricultural rates for all foreign shipments, and maintaining higher rates on those of a domestic character. This disposition on the part of the government to shield the interests of the agriculturists in the older and longer cultivated regions of European Russia, against a too violent competition created by the free use of property common to all, can be reckoned with as one of the influences that will limit and control the rapidity with which the lands of Siberia will be occupied and reclaimed.

Another restraint upon the rapid occupation of these lands lies in the tenure of a rather sparse but evenly distributed Tartar element. Unlike our American Indians, who possessed the waste lands of the West and lived exclusively by the chase, the Tartars who spread over the greater portion of Western Siberia are of a pastoral character, having immense herds of domestic animals in great variety; they will, therefore, hold the lands occupied by their ancestors from time immemorial with greater tenacity, a juster right, and firmer tenure. To dispossess them, therefore, will not be the easy problem that it was in the case of our own Aborigines.

In view of these deterrent causes, it is not likely that the lands of Siberia will be occupied and developed in the quick and wholesale manner witnessed in our own and other new countries, even though the Russian government were desir-

TOWN ON THE VOLGA RIVER

ous of following our example, a not probable contingency.

As the Russian is probably the most prolific race on the globe, an abundant supply of land must be kept available to meet this current want, since the cultivable lands of European Russia are already closely worked up. The present increase of population is reckoned at 2,000,000 per annum, which at the same ratio will be swelled to 3,000,000 within another generation. As the unit requirement must be estimated at about four or five acres per capita, there is, therefore, in sight an annual requirement of from 8,000,000 to 12,000,000 acres to supply this want, the annual reclamation of which will be in itself an achievement of no ordinary character.

Having due regard, therefore, for the variety of restraining influences and home necessities, and while in certain localities there may be at times excessive production, it does not seem probable that the surplus from this region, taken during a period of average production, will so far outrun the increased demand due to increased population as to leave such a residuum for export as will have any sensible effect upon western prices.

XII

Russian life in Siberia—Visiting various villages—Siberian towns and villages—Mostly frame or log houses—Efforts at ornamentation—Number and appointment of rooms—Clothing of the natives—The icon—The Russian peasant most religious—In the peasant's home—A mark of respect never to be omitted—Custom of recognizing the icon in Russia universal—Fare of the peasant—A singular bathroom—The drink of the peasant—Two kinds of quass—Vodka, its use and effects—Salutary regulations by the government—Worthy of imitation by other nations—Siberia the land of the exile—Erroneous impression of the traveller—Courtesy of Russian officials—Abolition of serfdom—Its effects contrasted with abolition of slavery in America—Administration of justice—Respect for law and authority—Difficulties encountered by Russia in its development—Obstacles to its progress—Remarkable national development—Banishment of bank officials to Siberia—Their status during and after term of sentence—Punished for fraud at gaming—Not a good country for irregular practices—Passport system—Citizens of Russia required to have passport—Registration of same, fee, etc.—Effects of the passport system—Special passport required to leave Russia—Beneficial results of same.

Having a desire to become familiar with the life of the lower class of Russians in Siberia, remote from the influences that centre about lines of railway, while in Tomsk I made a journey into the interior on the route to Tobolsk, which in a general way follows the valley of the Obi. This

SIBERIAN TOWNS

led me through many villages of a more or less primitive and interesting character.

These Siberian towns are, exclusively, mere assemblages of farm-houses with the usual build-

VILLAGE IN SIBERIA, BETWEEN TOMSK AND THE YENISEI RIVER

ings for stock, etc., and are in all respects similar to their prototypes in European Russia. With few exceptions, the dwellings and outhouses are built of logs, obtained from the strip of forest that fringes most of the rivers. Excepting in the large towns and railway stations. I do not believe I saw a single building of stone or brick. Being constructed generally with high, steep roofs, heavy cornices, and deep projections, with other crude efforts at ornamentation, they very often combine a pleasing external effect with much internal convenience and comfort, being as a rule warm in winter and cool in summer.

The houses are usually of three rooms: the kitchen, dining-room, and bed-room, the latter used also as a reception-room. They have plain wooden floors, and the furniture is of the simplest kind and very limited.

One thing I noticed especially: that, while the clothing was coarse, the people were always warmly clad, the men invariably wearing high-top boots, made generally of leather, but often of a thick felt, always coming well up to the knee.

In every house, without exception, one discovers in the corner of each room the ever-present little gilt icon, for be it remembered that the strongest trait of the Russian's character is his intense religious sentiment. Unlike many other countries, where it too often becomes a mere formula and even a convenience, with the Russian peasant especially it is a part of his life, the very essence, in fact, of his inner being. What is not the least surprising fact is, that the men are even more

HOUSES IN SMALL SIBERIAN TOWN, ON THE POST-ROAD TO TOBOLSK

punctilious in their observance of the formalities of the church than the women.

Although fairly comfortable lodging can be had at any of the post-houses on the main roads,

DWELLING-HOUSE IN SIBERIAN VILLAGE, ON POST-ROUTE FROM HAGA TO TOMSK

I, however, preferred to stop in the humble dwellings of the peasants, whose doors are always open to the stranger, with a rude though sincere hospitality.

On entering a dwelling it is a mark of respect,

never to be omitted, to courteously recognize the sacred icon that always hangs conspicuously on the wall. This is so universal a custom that, through-

SIBERIAN VILLAGE IN OBI VALLEY

out Russia everywhere, in all public buildings, stores, banks, counting-houses, etc., the men invariably uncover their heads before the icon, and so remain even while transacting business. Religion, therefore, in this country is carried contin-

LIFE OF THE PEASANT

nously right into the active, busy current of human affairs and life.

I noticed that, on entering a dwelling, the housewife at once went to a large chest and took out a carpet, which she spread carefully on the usually

NEW VILLAGE IN THE VALLEY OF THE TOM RIVER, SIBERIA

bare floor, and which seems to be reserved for important occasions. The samovar is at once set before you, as all Russians are inveterate tea drinkers. The tea is of a good quality, coming from China, and usually compressed in the form of small bricks.

The fare of the peasant is simple but wholesome, usually of rye bread, though often of the most excellent wheaten variety, with splendid soups and meats. On account of the abundance of pasturage in Siberia, meats of all kinds come readily within reach of the common people. The best quality of beef can be had anywhere on the Siberian railway for a little over two cents per pound. Large, fine bullocks ready for the market can be purchased for twenty to thirty rubles, or twelve to eighteen dollars. A first-class milk cow brings only eight to fifteen rubles. A pair of young chickens, five to ten cents. A brace of excellent ducks, much like our blue-winged teal, can be had for ten cents, and at the railway restaurants nicely roasted for eighteen cents apiece.

In almost every peasant dwelling a large baking oven is to be found at one end of the kitchen, made of thick walls of brick or some sort of cement composite. As it usually seemed of needless size, and the door out of proportion also, and instead of the usual dome form was flat on top, my attention was so attracted that I was led to inquire the purpose of these peculiarities. I was informed that it was not only used for baking purposes, but quite often served as a hot bath as well, straw being spread on the oven floor—previously heated by fagots burned within—for the protection of the bather, who crawls into the open door. By

FARE OF THE PEASANT

pouring water on the heated floor, it could thus be quickly changed from a hot-air to a vapor bath. During the winter, bedding is spread on the flat top of the oven, and, by maintaining a slow fire within, a comfortable warmth is imparted even in nights of extreme cold.

Besides tea, the peasants drink large quantities of a beverage called quass. Of this there are two varieties, one extracted from a small berry much like the cranberry, that grows in a wild state in the greatest abundance. The juice of this berry is allowed to slightly ferment, producing a most delicious and wholesome drink. Being so abundantly produced, it sells for only a few copecks a bottle, and is therefore universally used.

Another variety of quass is made by passing hot water through toasted bread and allowing it to slightly ferment. This is in great request by the peasantry, being a most wholesome and not unpleasant drink.

Vodka, here as in every part of Russia, is much used by all classes and both sexes, old and young. It is distilled from grain. Being of strong alcoholic properties, it is highly intoxicating, and it is somewhat remarkable that drunkenness is not far more prevalent, considering the immense quantity consumed in Russia. Except in the larger cities, such as St. Petersburg and Moscow, cases of intoxication are not more frequently met with than in Anglo-Saxon communities.

While hastily referring to the local and personal proclivities and habits of these people, it may be well to briefly glance at some more general practices and customs, the result of salutary regulations by the government.

At every station on the Siberian railway—which, I believe, is true to some extent on all Russian railways—there is placed in front of the station, at a point convenient of access by the passengers, a large cask of cool water, that has been thoroughly boiled, and it is the duty of the station-master to see that a liberal supply is kept up. This is free to all passengers, even to the poorest emigrant, whose comfort and welfare are provided for in many ways with thoughtful care.

In addition, an immense samovar is also placed in front of the station, which is kept full of boiling water for the use of the passengers on the trains. As they almost always carry a supply of tea with them, they are, therefore, enabled at any time to secure hot water, which they take into the train, and thus can make the desired quantum of tea at their leisure.

I am also informed that in large cities like St. Petersburg, where the water is not of the purest, it is the duty of every householder, during the summer, to place a suitable vessel in front of his house, containing boiled water, for the free use of the passerby. The contents of the vessel must be changed daily. If, upon inspection by the proper

CASK OF WATER AT STATION ON SIBERIAN RAILWAY, SUPPLIED WITH BOILED WATER FOR USE OF PASSENGERS

authorities, a supply is found wanting, or, upon analysis, it proves impure, the delinquent is severely punished.

Were such wise regulations in the general interest and welfare adopted by some other nations who lay claim to advantages of a superior civilization, we might hear less of "Maidstone epidemics."

So much has been written about Siberia, "the land of the exile," and so many gruesome pictures drawn of the horrors of Russian official tyranny, that to the uninitiated Siberia seems a dark, forbidding, and forbidden land; so that the newly arrived traveller almost instinctively grasps his passport at the very sight of a Russian official.

Fairness and candor compel me to say, however, that in no country in which I have travelled have I seen in the same time so little interference by the authorities with the current life and daily affairs of the people. In fact, I do not believe there exists in any nation a body of officials more considerate and courteous, or who are more attentive to the wishes and interests of the people, from the highest to the lowest station in life.

The time was, doubtless, when an undue espionage and the exercise of what was perhaps a despotic authority were deemed essential for the preservation of the government and general order, under which wrongs and even cruel practices may have arisen. But it must be remembered that scarcely more than one generation has passed since one-half of her population was suddenly changed from a servile class into free and independent citizens, with newly-acquired power and interests, and along with them new duties and obligations.

It is easy to see that a confusion resulting from a sudden transition that inverted an ancient political and social structure, might give rise to such conditions as to render even a stern exercise of authority a necessity. The wonder is, that any nation could survive a shock so violent and extreme, whatever might be its efforts to repress and control and hold in check the forces of dissolution and disintegration.

To realize fully the difficulties arising from changes so rapid and fundamental, we have but to recall the newly-created problems and difficulties in our own country—which are unfortunately still far from a final solution—growing out of the enfranchisement of a relatively few slaves. We may also be inclined to judge less severely other nations for their short-comings if we bring to remembrance the wrongs perpetrated by the Northern carpet-bag governments in the South during the days of reconstruction.

Within certain limits this is, perhaps, the most secure and the freest country in the world; for while the laws are rigorously executed and punishment is meted out with appalling certainty, the welfare and security of the people and government seem to be the prime motive in the minds of those who administer the law.

All trials are conducted with careful deliberation, and with an eye to secure and subserve strict justice. However needless and harsh the administration of justice in some cases may seem to be, it is certain that the swift, wholesale, and impartial execution of their salutary laws has established a condition of internal peace and security, creating respect for authority, and a recognition of just reciprocal rights that is truly wonderful, when all things are considered.

To realize this fully, we must take into account the vast extent of the country, the heterogeneous races that go to make up this great ethnical composite, with their respective rights, customs, traditions, castes, and vested interests—the outgrowth of thousands of years of racial development—all going to make up a vast mosaic of powerful and conflicting races, with almost irreconcilable antagonisms and interests.

Perhaps no nation has ever had to encounter, to the same extent, those impediments to progress and stable growth arising out of the necessity of tearing down the old in order to build up the new—a dilemma so well defined by the saying that "the good stands in the way of the better." In no nation, perhaps, has the problem of uniting a just government and liberal institutions with the impulse of modern change and progress been so difficult of solution as in this great empire. That under these adverse conditions she has been enabled to make that remarkable advance witnessed in the last two generations, stands as a marvel in the history of national development.

This is brought to our minds with increased force when we recall the fact that even so small and compact a country as the United Kingdom, where a great and steady advance has long been made in industrial, commercial, and political life, ancient rights and interests and traditions have not as yet been reconciled with the newer order of things, nor have its integral parts been welded into a harmonious whole, as the present state of Ireland shows.

On my way to Tomsk there were, among the passengers on the train, a man and wife, both of them respectable in appearance and accomplished. Although having the liberty of the train, their movements seemed under restraint, and an official was always hovering conveniently near. In a few days I learned that the man was on his way to Tomsk to serve out a ten years' banishment. He was formerly teller in a large bank in St. Petersburg, which failed disastrously some years ago, and he had improperly used some of its funds. Having been found guilty, after a searching trial lasting over two years, he was banished to Siberia for a term of ten years.

While he will be allowed his liberty in that city, he will not be permitted, during that time, to go beyond its precincts. The governor of the province can, at his discretion, transport him at any time to the most remote and obscure corner of his government. He will be allowed no social privileges whatever, and the grace of the authorities will be assured only by his excellent behavior. During the term of his sentence he will be practically deprived of all the rights and privileges of citizenship, and not allowed to engage in any business whatever. His business and social status after the expiration of his sentence will depend entirely upon his conduct in the meanwhile.

After the completion of the term of his banishment he will never be permitted to visit St. Petersburg, Moscow, or any other large city, seaport, or frontier town of the empire, and his subsequent engagement in business will depend wholly upon the decision of the authorities.

The other officials of this unfortunate bank, some fifteen in number, comprising among them many men of great wealth and highest social position, were, in virtue of their more important official relation to the bank, adjudged more highly culpable. They were, therefore, punished with corresponding rigor and severity. They were banished to various points in Siberia for a term of eighteen years. As many of them were of an advanced age, this was, in most cases, tantamount to a life sentence. The banishment of several was supplemented by two or three years at hard labor, which in Russia has a dismal significance. One was sent to Omsk, another to Tobolsk, and the rest scattered through Siberia in more or less wretched places, according to the degree of their crime. One, presumably the chief offender, was sent to Yakutsk, right in the heart of polar Siberia, said to be the coldest and dreariest place on the globe. As in the case that came under my notice, these condemned officials, even after the expiration of their sentence, will not be permitted to enter or visit any large city or frontier town, and cannot again engage in business, excepting by the grace of the authorities—a scant privilege that will even depend upon their deportment while serving their sentence.

Stopping on my return westward at a town on the Volga, in European Russia, I went to a hotel to await the arrival of the steamer that was to take me down that river. As this house was a large one and well appointed, and as there seemed much disorder in its management, I inquired the cause; and was informed that the proprietor, a man of much wealth, influence, and social position, had just been sentenced to ten years' banishment to Siberia, one year of which was at hard labor. Having departed on his melancholy journey only a few days before, the disordered state I discovered was accounted for.

On inquiry as to the nature of the crime he had committed, and for which he was convicted and so severely punished, I was astounded to learn that it was for cheating at cards at the gaming-table.

From these instances, I gathered the impression that Russia would not be a healthy place for the Hooleys of England and the professional wreckers of our own country to ply their profitable vocation of extracting money from the pockets of a confiding and trusting public, nor for the respectable gentlemen who so deftly lift their neighbors' money at baccarat.

There is, perhaps, no country in the world where the passport system is so deeply grounded, or where it is so thoroughly carried into effect as in Russia. Not only is it essential, in order to gain admission into this country, that every foreigner be fortified by a passport issued by his government, but even every citizen of Russia is required to possess one and keep it conveniently at hand.

They are issued to Russian citizens for one year, and must be promptly renewed annually.

The cost is from five to twenty-five rubles, according to the class. No one, not even a citizen of Russia, can go from one city or locality to another with the intention of remaining twenty-four hours without showing his passport.

No sooner does one arrive at a hotel, be he native or stranger, than his passport is called for. It is taken to the public headquarters and the necessary registry made, for which a registration fee of ten cents is required. Should any one find himself in any city other than his own place of residence even for twenty-four hours without a passport, he is at once detained by the police until a satisfactory explanation is forthcoming. If satisfaction can be given and proof of good citizenship be presented, a new passport is supplied; otherwise the police take permanent charge of the delinquent and his case is disposed of by a more or less severe punishment.

It is thus that the government can keep a complete record of all its citizens, and a close watch on their movements. It is, moreover, an instrument that greatly aids in more thoroughly utilizing all its sources of energy, and in knitting more effectively together the potencies of national life into a compact, mobile whole, leaving no loose ends floating about.

As a passport is required to gain admission into Russia, so is one essential to gain permission to leave the country. Every one, foreigner or citizen, is obliged to show this passport on arrival at the frontier before he is permitted to depart from Russia. Under these conditions, it is well nigh impossible for any one in this country to pull a bank or wreck a railroad, and then conveniently skip over the border to enjoy his ill-gotten gains in other lands.

XIII

Passenger boats on the Caspian Sea—New lines of steamers—Petrovsk, on the Caspian—Excursion into the mountains—New railway line to Baku—Great through line to Central Asia—Important influence of the Trans-Caspian railway upon this world's affairs—Extension of same into China—Distance and time by this route to China—Direct and short route to Northern India—Projected line of railway from Orenburg to Tashkent—Ambitions of Russia in a new field—Great canal between the Black Sea and the Baltic—Great commercial and strategic importance of same—Steady and persistent progress of Russia—Her advance not rapid, but secure—Does not vaunt her enterprises—Effects upon political world of Trans-Caspian railway to be greater than the Trans-Siberian railway—New route from Merv to Herat—Its probable influence on Afghanistan—Projected lines into Persia—Line being built from Armenia to Northern Persia—Important results to arise therefrom in that country—New line projected from Samarkand southward to Karshi—That city the key to Northeastern Afghanistan—Possibility of formidable attack of Russia upon Northern India via Central Asia—No combination of powers could stay it—Unimportant part naval forces would play in such a contest—Russia's contiguous territory and interior operations a manifest advantage—Such a conflict might require the whole power of Great Britain to repel—Russia's peace proposal—Her sincerity in same—Prefers peaceful methods to those of war—Her superior strategical position—May not Russia's evident advantage over India operate to preserve peace?—The fortunate position of America in the event of a great Asiatic war.

SAMARKAND, CENTRAL ASIA, *October*, 1898.

BESIDES numerous steam and sail vessels that carry on a large freight traffic on the Caspian Sea, there are several excellent lines of passenger boats, the chief one being the Kavkaz and Mercury line. This company is constantly adding new and well-equipped steamers to accommodate

THE GREAT PETROLEUM CITY OF BAKU, ON THE CASPIAN SEA IN THE EASTERN CAUCASUS. VIEW FROM THE BAY.

its rapidly increasing travel and traffic. The steamers of this line call at the larger Russian towns on the Caspian Sea, and also at those of Persia, on its southern border.

GENERAL VIEW OF THE CITY OF BAKU

The past year they have added to their fleet two screw vessels of about two thousand tons, fitted up with every modern convenience, and which readily make sixteen knots per hour. On one of these I embarked at Astrakhan for Baku, the chief port in the middle Caucasus.

The first stop is at Petrovsk, the district town of the Daghestan. Before reaching this city, the majestic range of the Caucasian Mountains, among the highest on the globe, rises into view, bearing away to the northwest, with the fine snow-capped peak of the great Kazbek just peeping above the horizon. The boat stopping here several hours, gives an opportunity to make a pleasant excursion into the foot-hills of the Daghestan Mountains, a trip well rewarded by what one sees among the wild, rude tribes that people this rugged region.

Petrovsk, like many other towns under the influence of Russian enterprise, is growing rapidly; and in virtue of its excellent port, as well as the position it occupies as an important intermediate point on the soon-to-be through Trans-Caspian and Central Asian route, it is destined to become a city of much importance.

There is now a railroad running from Petrovsk to Moscow, via Vladikavkaz and Rostoff on the Don, and the journey can be most comfortably made without change in three days on a splendid through train, a distance of nearly two thousand miles.

A road is almost completed, running along the shore of the Caspian Sea to Baku, a distance of

CATHEDRAL IN BAKU

300 miles. This is designed to connect with the line of steamers running across the Caspian Sea from the western terminus of the Trans-Caspian railway to Baku, making thus a direct line running

from Central Asia to Moscow, and thence to Western Europe.

I have heretofore pointed out that results of the utmost commercial, industrial, and even ethical importance to Northern and Eastern China, as well as to the world generally, must speedily follow the completion of the great Trans-Siberian railway, with its contemplated tributaries projecting southward into China.

In anticipation of the facts, which I will hereafter give more in detail, of the development of Russian Central Asia, I would say that by a like policy of railway extension in that country results even more far-reaching in their importance to Southern and Western, and especially to Middle China, Northern India, Afghanistan, and Persia, will follow the completion of the main line of the Trans-Caspian railway, with its tributaries radiating into those countries. At the present rapid rate of advance, this will be realized at no distant day.

The Trans-Caspian railway is now practically completed from Krasnovodsk, on the eastern shore of the Caspian Sea, to Tashkent, the capital of Turkestan, near the China border, a distance of about 1,200 miles. With the exception, therefore, of the transit across the Caspian Sea, a continuous trip will soon be possible from Paris, or any part of Western Europe, to the northern confines of India and right up to the western border of China.

The time now required on the Trans-Caspian railway is three days. It can, however, easily be shortened to two. The Caspian Sea may be crossed in fifteen hours. The distance between Baku and Moscow can in future be covered in less than three days; so that within a year it will be possible to make the journey from Western China to Moscow within six days.

Following this idea further, it will be among the possibilities within the next decade to go from Paris to Kokand, or Kashgar, or the central northern border of India, or even to Central China, within from ten days to two weeks. As the time now required to go from London or Paris to Northern India via Marseilles, the Mediterranean Sea, Suez, and the Indian Ocean is over three weeks, and the cost more than double, some conception can be formed of the great changes that in future are to be wrought in the trade and travel between Northern India, Central Asia, China, and European countries, when the possibilities of this great highway are fully realized.

By a projection of this route from Tashkent into Central China, that vast region could be so linked with Central Europe that ten or twelve days might suffice for the journey. As by no

RAILWAY STATION IN BAKU

other possible route could that vast region be joined to Europe in less than double the time and twice the expense, it becomes apparent how much in future Russia will control the destiny and material well-being of all Asia.

The Russian government has under contemplation the construction of yet another line, which, when completed, will form an additional and most important route between far Asiatic and European countries. At Samara, on the Volga, a branch line separates from the main stem of the Trans-Siberian railway, running to Orenburg in Southeastern Russia. It is the purpose of the government to extend this line southeastward some 1,200 miles (around the Aral Sea), following up the Syr-Daria—the ancient Jaxartes—to the very centre of Turkestan. By this line, a direct and continuous all-rail communication will be established between Northern Central Asia, Central China, and Europe.

Having practically realized the most stupendous railway enterprise ever undertaken, Russia now seems ambitious to achieve an equally important and brilliant success in another field. It is nothing less than the formidable project to connect the Black Sea and the Baltic by a gigantic waterway.

This is to be accomplished through uniting, by

great canals, the various rivers flowing through the wide and intervening country, a distance of 600 or 800 miles. They are to be constructed of such unusual size and capacity that, in addition to the vast commercial purposes they will serve, they will also be used for the transit of her naval armament from one sea to the other, securing thus, through her own territory, free communication, independent of any international route.

In other words, she will by this means secure for herself in European Russia those exclusive strategical advantages which the Trans-Siberian and Trans-Caspian railways have already given her in Asiatic countries. This great project has not as yet assumed a tangible shape, but that it will ultimately be carried out there can be little doubt, since this great nation has a way of realizing quietly and without ostentation, yet stubbornly and persistently, the vast schemes she conceives, despite all jealous cavil and opposition.

The boldness of conception, followed by a persistent and steady realization, of schemes of improvement and development so vast and daring, ill accords, I am sure, with the somewhat prevalent idea that Russia is a non-progressive, inert, or at least semi-passive nation.

Imbued to some extent with this notion, it is needless to say that in all my travels I have met

GROWTH OF COMMERCE AND TRADE 273

with few greater surprises than that of the steady and in many cases rapid advance in all directions of Russian industrial and commercial life.

It is true that she has not, as it has too often occurred in other nations in their strife and mad craze for excessive growth and progress, developed new, needless, and in many cases even injurious wants, nor has she anticipated for generations real necessities, all of which has had the effect of imparting in a large measure to such nations an air of fiction and inflation to their national life.

Fairness compels one to say that wherever, in due course and by natural growth, real wants and necessities arise, she meets them with commendable celerity and thoroughness. Her policy seems to be that of fully supplying those needs that naturally arise and develop, rather than following the example of other nations, the volume of whose trade and industries largely consists in supplying unnatural and superfluous wants, artificially created.

Nor is it her custom to herald abroad her proposed enterprises, or magnify the results when completed. Indeed, on the contrary, in some cases, such as her present developments in Central Asia, she discourages, and even represses, attempts to record them; and it is only the favored few who gain access to this almost unknown region who acquire any knowledge of the really wondrous changes that are now taking place in it.

Great as will be the effect upon the world of the opening of the Trans-Siberian railway system—a fact that is gradually being recognized—the Trans-Caspian railway system, when completed, will be productive of results even far more important in their political and commercial consequences.

There is a branch of the Trans-Caspian railway now completed, some 250 miles in length and running southward from Merv to Kushk, on the very borders of Afghanistan. It is being quietly extended to Herat, and it will, when completed, give Russia practical control of Northwestern Afghanistan, as Herat is the key to that country. This line is also projected to run further southward, through the heart of Persia down to the Persian Gulf,—very extensive concessions, as I learn, having recently been given to Russia by the Persian Government to build railways in that country. The railway that has just been constructed from Tiflis, in the Caucasus, to Alexandropol and Erivan in Armenia, is to be pushed down the Araxes River to Tibriz, Teheran, and Ispahan, thus crossing in the centre of Persia, almost at right angles, the branch line of the Trans-Caspian railway running southward from

Merv via Herat. These lines, when in operation, will thus obviously give Russia a controlling influence in Persia and Northwestern Afghanistan. A branch, also, of the main stem of the Trans-Caspian line is being built from Samarkand through Ferghan, in the direction of Kokand and Kashgar, in the Pamirs, almost in sight of the northern border of India. This line in time will, no doubt, be extended into Chinese Turkestan, and perhaps into the very centre of China itself, bringing thus this great and populous country into communication with Europe, even more directly than by the way of the Trans-Siberian railway line. Still another most important route is projected to run southward from Samarkand some 250 miles, through Southern Bokhara, to Karshi, on the northwestern confines of Afghanistan, and said to occupy one of the most important strategical positions in all Asia. Karshi lies but a short distance northeast of Balk, which place was the base of Alexander's operations against India, and from which he made his descent upon that country. An extension of this line further on, toward Candahar—a quite probable thing, as the Ameer of Afghanistan is said to be most favorably inclined to Russia—would give Russia practical control of the Cabul basin and of the northern half of Afghanistan. As the

Trans-Caspian railway and its tributaries, running to the very borders of India and through hundreds of miles distance, could be used if desired by Russia wholly for military operations against that country, it is apparent that she could inaugurate a movement in case of necessity against England's cherished possessions, of the most formidable and dangerous character. By her ample railway facilities, she could in a brief time throw along hundreds of miles of assailable frontier, myriads of soldiers, the best in the world, where they could readily be maintained as a perpetual menace to India. Nor does it seem possible for any combination of forces to prevent or arrest such a movement on the part of Russia, as no array of naval power could avail against the use of this system of railways as a military instrument, lying as it does in the very heart of the great Slavic empire, and far remote from the sea. As Russia is pushing her projected improvements in these regions steadily and with vigor, it is not improbable that she already feels that she controls the destinies of Southwestern Asia, and, even more, that at her leisure she can dictate to England what her future relations to that country shall be. If, unfortunately, hostilities should again arise between these two great powers, be the point of contact Port Arthur or Sebastopol, it may not be the privilege of England, in the event of a serious conflict, to choose her vantage ground, as this advantage would lie rather with Russia. The indifference with which the latter might well look upon an approach by sea, would leave her free to throw an overwhelming force upon an interior point, and thus shift the scene of real conflict to a region where the great naval forces of her adversary would be relatively of little use. By reason of the self-contained and self-sustaining power of Russia; her vast, impenetrable, and wholly contiguous territory, now practically conterminous with hundreds of miles of India's northern border; a widely ramifying railway system beyond the reach of an enemy to interrupt, and providing ample means direct for transportation of troops and supplies, it seems probable that such an assault could be made by her upon India (that might be prolonged indefinitely) as would require the entire resources of England to meet and at the same time to preserve the peace of her none too loyal subjects there, whose discontent would find a stimulus in the near presence of a powerful ally. May we not find in a situation so exceptional, a position so obviously commanding and assured, the true significance of Russia's recent peace proposals?

May it not in reality suggest a generous desire on her part to aid in securing those measures whereby the world's great powers shall voluntarily delimit their ambitions, and thus assure the future integrity of trade and commerce? For, with the most powerful army on the globe, and holding a position of such rare strategical advantage, of which she is doubtless fully conscious, is it likely that she entertains any fear of the issue of a contest with any possible combination, under conditions now so distinctly in her favor?

It is an interesting question, well worthy of consideration, how far this manifest tactical advantage enjoyed by Russia will in future operate to maintain peace, or will even conduce to an ultimate friendly relation of the two great powers, between whom it is difficult to discern other than a common interest, or at least any substantial cause to perpetuate hostile relations.

If unfortunately a collision should arise on the lines here pointed out, with its destructive effects, its widespread disaster to the trade, commerce, and industry of all European and Asiatic peoples, our own country will have cause for congratulation that, by the fortunate position it occupies, she will escape the deplorable consequences that are certain to grow out of the entangling relations and alliances that harass and plague less fortunate nations.

GENERAL VIEW OF THE CITY AND HARBOR OF BAKU

XIV

The great city of Baku—Its rapid growth—Cause of same—Yet growing rapidly—The petroleum deposits in the Caucasus—Number of wells in operation—Limited exploration of Caucasian oil fields—New field north of the Caucasian range of mountains—Output of the oil wells in 1897—Stories current in Baku—A lucky Tartar—Wonderful wells—Refineries in "Black Town," near Baku—Crude oil extensively used as fuel in Southern Russia—Desire to visit Central Asia—Importance of that country politically—The key to India, Western China, and perhaps Constantinople—Intricacies of European politics—India the real storm centre—India indispensable to England's power and greatness—Her anxiety and efforts to preserve same—Her fear of Russia's designs upon India—Has relied upon her great navy—Her naval strength would avail but little to check Russia's advance through Central Asia—Russia's railway building in Asia regarded as a menace to India—The "gospel of the machine"—Russian railway advance in Asia—Desire for alliances—The open door—Cautious measures of Russia in her Central Asian possessions.

Among the many almost miraculous creations of modern trade and industry, Baku deserves to take a conspicuous place in the list of phenomenal cities. In its ante-petroleum days it was merely one of many small and even insignificant towns that dotted the Caucasian shore of the Caspian Sea, at which an occasional sail vessel called for the purposes of local trade. It is to-day a great city of 150,000 inhabitants, with large and beautiful business blocks, many well-paved streets, tramways, electric lights, telephone system, etc.; and its capa-

OIL FIELD SOUTH OF BAKU, NEAR THE SHORE OF THE CASPIAN SEA, OPERATED BY ENGLISH AND FRENCH CAPITALISTS

cious harbor is literally jammed with sail and steam vessels, its commerce extending to the remotest limits of the empire, and even far into Europe.

It is the familiar story of a newly discovered

resource, so great as to cause the convergence of the world's energy and capital upon it. The primary cause of its rapid growth is, of course, the great petroleum interests of which it is the centre. But a great accession of trade and energy grows out of the fact that Baku is in reality the western terminus of the Trans-Caspian railway, the commercial forces and influences of which impinge full upon this fortunate city.

Rapid as has been the growth of this queer city in recent years, there seems to be no abatement in the rate of its expansion, for everywhere great stone and brick edifices are being now erected, new streets laid out, and the old Persian, Tartar, and Armenian quarters, if not literally razed to build a new city upon, at least newly traversed by broad and elegant avenues.

Nor does there seem to be a probability of an early limit to its rapid growth, since the petroleum interests of this region are as yet hardly more than explored. It seems to be the opinion of many scientists that the petroleum deposits of the Eastern Caucasus are the most important on the globe.

As yet only two fields have been developed, one lying about two miles south of the city, near the sea level, and containing about 500 wells; the other some six miles north of the city, and at an elevation of several hundred feet above the level of the sea, containing about 1,200 wells. In all, therefore, there are at present some 1,800 wells tributary to Baku.

OIL FIELD NORTHWEST OF BAKU, SEVERAL HUNDRED FEET ABOVE THE SEA LEVEL, OPERATED BY SWEDISH AND FRENCH CAPITALISTS

The first mentioned field is being largely worked by English capital, and the latter by Noebel, the Swedish discoverer of dynamite, and the

Rothschilds. New wells are being sunk in great numbers, and the road from Baku to the northern field, a distance of six miles, is almost literally impassable, so crowded is it with teams hauling great boilers and other machinery destined for the use of new wells or those in course of preparation.

But comparatively little testing has been done to determine the true extent of the oil fields of the Caucasus, but enough to establish the fact that they cover the greater portion of the Eastern Caucasus and extend even into Northern Persia. Quite a promising field has been opened the past three or four years on the northern slope of the Caucasian Mountains, midway between Petrovsk and Vladikavkaz.

From Baron von der Hoven, the head of the statistical department for Eastern Caucasus, I learned that this industry was rapidly on the increase. The output of crude oil last year was nearly 2,000,000,000 gallons. In 1891 there were fifteen refineries, producing 80,000,000 gallons of refined oil.

The same marvellous stories are current here of the sudden transition from extreme poverty to great wealth, that embellished the history of Western Pennsylvania in the "Coal Oil Johnny" days. You are told of the wretchedly poor Armenian or lucky Tartar, the possessor of a tract of land so miserably sterile that a whole acre would not yield subsistence for a handful of grasshoppers, who found himself suddenly possessed of wealth beyond the dreams of avarice.

A Tartar was pointed out to me who a few years ago was pounding stone on the street for a living, and is now said to be worth 25,000,000 rubles.

The interested traveller is also expected to be astonished by the usual stories about the wonderful performance of some spouter or gusher that has broken the record. I was shown a well belonging to the Rothschilds, which while now only an ordinary producer, is said to have once spouted for months at a time at the astounding rate of nearly 2,000,000 gallons a day.

Along the bay, in the northeast part of the city, are located the large refineries of Noebel and the Rothschilds, which alone have created quite a city, called " Black Town."

This immense deposit of oil is destined to be a source of great wealth to Russia. Besides supplying a large quantity for export, it is used in a crude form for fuel throughout much of the empire. The steamboats on the Don, Volga, and other rivers, on the Caspian Sea, and to some extent also in the Black Sea, as also almost all the railways in Southeastern Russia, use the crude oil exclusively for fuel.

A CELEBRATED SPOUTER

I confess that for years I have cherished an ardent desire to visit Central Asia and the ancient cities of Merv, Bokhara, and Samarkand, about which to my youthful imagination such a halo of romance was thrown by Alexander the Great, and which, in more modern times, was the seat of that mighty Tartar power under Zinghiz Khan and Tamerlane; a region, too, that once was so famous in the annals of literature and of art.

The vague expectation of being able to obtain a permit to see this interesting country was one of the incentives to my visiting the Caspian region at this time. Perhaps no country, excepting some portions of China, has been so long excluded from the world, and into which admission was so difficult, as Central Asia. Indeed, the Bokharian portion of it records but one authenticated visit by a European previous to this century, and it is only in comparatively recent years that other than a few Russian officials have gone into this sealed land.

Great as was the part that Central Asia played in the past in the world's affairs, she seems destined to play indirectly the same rôle in scarcely a less degree, since it is fast becoming the key to Western China and Southern Asia, Afghanistan and Persia, and may even yet point the way to Constantinople.

To those at all familiar with the intricacies of

European politics, and who study its delicate adjustments, it is apparent that no matter what disturbance of the political atmosphere there may be in the Balkans, on the Nile, in Turkey, or Palestine, or even the Baltic, for the most part the real storm centre can be sought for and found in India.

England, it seems, has come to regard the retention of that country as synonymous with her national prosperity and supremacy, and, in truth, were she to lose it, she would at once descend to a second-rate power. In view of this, for a century she has artfully contrived to create and maintain a system of national checkmates in Europe, to safeguard her Indian possessions and subserve her cherished purposes elsewhere. Whatever might be the aims, desires, and abilities of other nations, she has chosen to regard Russia as her natural enemy, and the one nation filled with a covetous desire for this her choicest possession.

The extreme sensitiveness displayed by this great nation—which upon all other questions preserves such an admirable equipoise—whenever Russia makes the least movement eastward, presents a strange spectacle. No matter what that nation may do, she seems to regard every incident and event, however remote, to which Russia is related, as a direct menace to India.

Every now and again, some apocryphal story

flashes athwart the British press about Russia's sinister designs in Central Asia. If it be reported that she is building a railway toward Herat or the Pamirs, a common road in the direction of Persia, or if some Russian officer should chance to turn his binoculars toward the Afghan mountains, fear seems to seize this stalwart nation, and a note of alarm is sounded that India is threatened.

Having long chosen to regard Russia as holding traditional designs on India, and having adopted the rather singular view that the Mediterranean was to be the road to that coveted land, it was this that caused her to create her immense naval armament to patrol that sea, as a means of insuring the safety of her Indian possessions. Now that Russia, by a system of railways in her own possessions, is approaching the very border of India, by which, if she chooses to do so, she can throw the weight of her empire against upper India, we can find in this new situation a reasonable excuse for England's present anxiety, seeing that her mighty ironclads, created at so much pains and at so great an expense, are likely to prove about as effective in preventing the approach of Russia in this more vulnerable direction, as so much old junk.

Into what strange and erratic courses such fear can lead a nation, in so many ways the greatest and most admirable, is signally illustrated by a recent occurrence. When the Czar made his late proposal of disarmament—a scheme so beneficent that it might well call down upon the head of the young ruler the praises and blessings of all lovers of peace and humanity—some of the leading papers of England, that direct and mould public sentiment, made the counter proposal, that before giving it consideration, Russia should be asked, as a pledge of her sincerity, to cease building railways in China and Central Asia.

This proposition, to say the least, is an astounding one, coming as it did from a nation that justifies its occupation of India, and the conquest of unoffending African races, mainly on the ground that these people will thereby receive the benefits of railways and other blessings of a new civilization.

Strangely enough, this "gospel of the machine" seems to be spreading apace, and may yet supplant that of the "meek and lowly." However sound it may seem to be in the abstract, or whatever may be the present results of its practical application, I doubt if the world is yet prepared to accept the full consequences of a doctrine so grossly material, as that the immunity of any nation from wanton and unprovoked assault by other nations is to be measured by its readiness to accept and its capacity to consume the modern products of the mine and the loom.

The many evidences during the past year of the rapidity with which Central Asia was being Russianized, and the equally rapid advance of her great railway towards an open seaport on the Pacific at Port Arthur, with its contemplated collateral branches into China, have in the past few months quickened England into increased efforts to check or obstruct the movements of her great adversary, which, however local or domestic they may in reality be, she regards as having an object personal to herself.

It is not the least singular fact in this connection that she seems to lack confidence in her own unaided abilities, as her search for alliances would appear to indicate. In her desire to compass this, with a rare inconsistency, the tempting bait of "open door trade" is proffered to nations who long have been, and are likely long to remain, irrevocably committed to a "closed door policy" far more rigid in character than that of Russia. Naturally enough, as a foil to these obstructive efforts, Russia retorts with protective measures of extreme caution and vigilance, even to placing a partial though temporary interdict upon her Central Asian possessions.

XV

Admission into Trans-Caspian country—Military railway—Special permit necessary in Trans-Caspian region—Across Northern Persia—On the Araxes River—First view of Mt. Ararat—Crossing the Araxes—Mt. Ararat—Grandeur of same—Ascent of Ararat—Armenian cemetery—Across the Araxes Valley—Erivan, the capital of Armenia—Mosques, palaces, etc.—Change under Russian rule—New railway line south of Erivan—Markets in Erivan—The great-tailed sheep—On the road to the Caucasus—Last view of Mt Ararat—Curious religious sects—Picturesque Lake of Goktcha—Height above the sea—The ancient monastery of Sevanga—Over the Delijan Pass—Descent of northern slope of Armenian mountains—Arrival at Akstafa on the Kura River.

MANY curious stories are afloat at Baku respecting the various attempts of would-be English tourists to gain admission into the Trans-Caspian country. Relying upon the sufficiency of their passports, they cross the Caspian Sea only to find themselves summarily and promptly sent back again. Having this in mind, I called upon the governor of Baku for permission to go over the Trans-Caspian railway to Samarkand and Tashkent.

I might add here that this railway is purely a military one, undertaken and built by Russia for

the purpose of securing her interests in Central
Asia, and is operated by the Ministry of War. I
was, however, informed at Merv that as soon as
the branches that are being built into Turkestan,
Feraghan, and to the Afghan border are com-

INTERIOR OF THE ANCIENT PALACE OF THE VICEROYS OF PERSIA IN
ERIVAN

pleted, the road will be handed over to the civil
authorities to be operated by the Ministry of Railways, becoming thus, like all other railroads in this
country, freely open to all, and to general trade
purposes. This is expected to be done within the
next year.

The official to whom I applied, while admitting the present extreme precautions of his government, replied that whatever limitations might be placed upon the movements of others, the American was always privileged and welcome to freely travel in any portion of the empire, merely upon the passport of his government. He, however, significantly added that to insure perfect freedom and unrestrained facilities for travel, it would be well to secure a special permit from the Minister of the Interior, he himself having no authority to issue one. This could be readily done, he assured me, by letter or personal application to the Minister at St. Petersburg. Finding that this would consume nearly a month, and not caring to undertake a trip so full of hardships, with no certainty of having the necessary freedom to see the desired objects of interest there, I reluctantly abandoned the journey.

Taking the boat for Lenkoran, 100 miles south of Baku, I crossed through Northern Persia to the Araxes River, which forms the boundary between that country and Russia. Following up this river, I reached the small town of Nakhchivan, which means in Persian "the first descent," and is supposed to be the first resting place of Noah, after leaving the ark. While there I was shown a veritable piece of the true ark, which I admired with much interest and becoming reverence.

Following the river mentioned, we passed the

CARAVAN CROSSING THE ARAXES RIVER, ON THE BORDERS OF RUSSIA AND PERSIA, EN ROUTE FOR ERIVAN, ARMENIA

little Ararat, a beautifully pointed mountain of 12,000 feet in height. The road follows somewhat closely the course of the Araxes, which, throughout much of its length, constitutes the boundary between Persia and Russia. This road is the great highway that joins Northern Persia to the Caucasus and Europe. At Kamerlu there is a branch road that leads westward to Aralykh, at

ON THE BANKS OF THE ARAXES RIVER, FORMING THE BOUNDARY BETWEEN RUSSIA AND PERSIA.

the base of the Great Ararat. This is a military post, where a great number of Cossacks are permanently quartered, and it is from this point that the ascent of Mt. Ararat is made. About midway

GROUP OF NATIVES AT KAMERLU

between Kamerlu and Aralykh, a distance of about ten miles, the Araxes River is crossed on a primitive ferry.

After that, we came upon the real Ararat of

IN THE VALLEY OF THE ARAXES RIVER. LITTLE AND GREAT ARARAT MOUNTAINS IN THE DISTANCE

Scripture and history, one of the most beautiful and stately of mountains, and about 17,000 feet in height. I have seen most of the celebrated mountains of the globe, but of them all none presents a more imposing appearance than Ararat, viewed from the Araxes that washes its very base. Most lofty mountains are so situated that

DISTANT VIEW OF MT. ARARAT

the summit can be seen only at a great distance, or else after much of its height has been reached. The summit of Ararat, however, can be seen from its very base, at a point only a few hundred feet

RUDE FERRY ACROSS THE ARAXES RIVER

above the level of the sea and at a distance as the bird flies of less than twenty miles.

The mountain, therefore, rises directly before you to a height of over three miles in a wonderfully impressive manner. By reason of its nearness, its perfect symmetry, the everlasting mantle of snow that envelops the summit, all viewed through the transparent atmosphere of this region, it becomes, perhaps, the most satisfactory mountain view on the globe.

The northern face has a very striking resemblance to that of Mount Etna, having a deep depression much like the *val del bove* of that mountain. I did not go to the summit, as it is a most fatiguing trip, requiring several days. As this region is infested with numerous and dangerous bands of brigands and robbers, those who visit the summit are provided by the government, for their protection, with ten or a dozen Cossacks from the barracks located at the foot of the mountain, where there are always quartered several regiments of these celebrated soldiers.

Soon after leaving the small town of Aghamzaly, I noticed at a short distance from the roadside quite a number of natives, dressed in varied costumes bright in their richness of colors. They were in an open space, literally covered with great round boulders scattered irregularly about.

On coming closer I discovered that it was a cemetery, and some important memorial service was being held. The stones, simply of a natural form and obtained from the hills nearby, served to mark the locality of the many graves. There was no enclosing wall or other protection for the cemetery. I was much impressed by the striking contrast of the rich, even gaudy, coloring of their costumes with the solemn occasion and sombre surroundings.

Cutting across the valley of the Araxes, we reached the ancient city of Erivan, the capital of Armenia. It is located on the Zanga River, an affluent of the Araxes, which it enters some twenty miles below, in the direction of Mt. Ararat. Erivan is full of half-ruined and what must have been exquisitely beautiful mosques, decayed palaces, ancient fortresses, and other reminders of its former Mohammedan masters. Many changes have occurred under Russian rule, greatly modernizing the city. Wide streets, spacious parks, handsome public buildings, Christian churches, etc., attest the presence of a new master.

On my way northward, I noticed the government was busily engaged in surveying a railway line down the valley of the Araxes. Persia is, no doubt, the southern objective point of this road, and it seemed to be heading for Tibriz. As Rus-

ON THE ROAD TO MT. ARARAT

sia has recently received from Persia extensive concessions, this, no doubt, is the initial line from the north into that country. This road is to join, at Alexandropol, the one now almost completed

COSSACK CAVALRYMEN ON THE ROAD TO MT. ARARAT

from Tiflis to that city. As the Trans-Caucasian railway runs from Tiflis to Batoum on the eastern shore of the Black Sea, this new line will ultimately form a continuous route from Central Persia to

Europe through Armenia, the Caucasus, and the Dardanelles. A future network of railways by Russia into Persia and Afghanistan will no doubt be a natural sequence to her network of railways in Central Asia.

While in Erivan I visited the markets there, of

RETURNING FROM MT. ARARAT

which there are several most important and highly interesting. The soil along the Zanga and Araxes rivers, being simply the washings or detritus of the enclosing volcanic mountains, is therefore of an extremely fertile nature. It much resembles the volcanic soils around Naples and in the vicinity of Mt. Vesuvius, being somewhat similarly formed.

VEGETABLE PRODUCTS OF ARMENIA   311

The many streams descending from the mountains give an abundant supply of water for irrigation, which is carried by a great network of canals and ditches throughout these rich and beautiful

PERSIAN CART OR AREA

valleys. Vegetables, therefore, not only grow there in the greatest profusion, but also in great variety. Almost every kind that is natural to a temperate climate can be found in the markets, and also many that are distinctly of a tropical nature.

I found there what was the finest specimen I have ever seen of that singular animal known as the "fat-tailed sheep," so often met with in African and Asiatic countries. Whether by gradual

MARKET SCENE IN ERIVAN. GREAT FAT-TAILED SHEEP

changes through domestication or by natural processes this extraordinary appendage has been developed, it is difficult to determine. It consists of two great lobes of fatty matter springing from the body of the animal on each side of the tail,

AN ARMENIAN CEMETERY

which is so completely embedded in it that it no longer possesses either the appearance or function of that useful member. So enormously is this peculiar growth developed in some cases that it al-

VIEW OF MT. ARARAT, LOOKING SOUTHWARD FROM ERIVAN, THE CAPITAL OF ARMENIA

most trails upon the ground. It is generally from 25 to 30 pounds in weight, but 40 to 50, and even 60, pounds are not uncommon. It is of an exceedingly delicate nature, more resembling marrow-fat than any other substance, and it is much prized for culinary purposes. It is largely used for soups throughout the country where the animal is bred, producing a most savory and agreeable article of

NEW MOSQUE OF HUSSEIN ALI KHAN IN ERIVAN

diet. This variety of sheep, besides being large and yielding an excellent kind of mutton, produces a heavy fleece of wool of fine quality.

Possessing so many desirable qualities, I have often wondered why some effort has not been made

STREET SCENE IN ERIVAN

to introduce it into our own country. It would, no doubt, be possible to do so, as it seems to adapt itself to almost all climatic and physical conditions, for I have met with it from the hot, arid plains of

ANCIENT MOHAMMEDAN MOSQUE IN ERIVAN

Nubia, Abyssinia, Egypt, and Central Asia, to the cold, humid atmosphere of the Himalayan and Altai mountains.

Taking the main road that leads in the direction

of Alexandropol, I reached, via the Delijan Pass and Lake Goktcha or Sevanga, the interesting and beautiful city of Tiflis, the capital of Georgia, pict-

A DUKOBORTSI VILLAGE—A RELIGIOUS SECT IN NORTHERN ARMENIA—ON THE ROAD FROM ERIVAN TO TIFLIS

uresquely located on the Kura River, directly in the midst of the Caucasian Mountains. The road after leaving Erivan passes through a highly volcanic region, being for the most part over ancient

REGIMENT OF COSSACKS ON THEIR WAY TO NORTHERN BORDER OF PERSIA, ON THE ARAXES RIVER

lava beds. At the distance of some thirty miles, we reach the summit of the mountain range that divides the valleys of the Zanga and Araxes rivers

THRESHING GRAIN IN ARMENIA. GRAIN IS TRODDEN OUT BY HORSES BEING DRIVEN OVER IT

from the more elevated plateau in the region of Elnofka.

From this summit we obtain our last view of Mt. Ararat, some sixty or seventy miles southward. The grand peaks of the Alagoz and Ak-Dagh, rising on either hand to the height of 14,000 and 12,000 feet respectively, lend some charm to the dreary aspect of this wild, desolate region. All along this route we passed with rapid frequency through the rude villages of the many singular religious sects scattered through this part

LITTLE ISLAND IN LAKE GOKTCHA, ON WHICH THE ANCIENT MONASTERY OF SEVANGA IS LOCATED

of Armenia; the Dukobortsi, Skoptsy, Molokani, etc.

At Elnofka we first meet the remarkably picturesque little lake of Goktcha, along whose rugged shores the road winds at a great elevation for some ten or twelve miles, until the Delijan Pass is reached. This lake is situated 7,000 feet above the sea. It is some forty miles in length and twenty in breadth. The trout caught here are

SKOPTSY VILLAGE—A PECULIAR RELIGIOUS SECT WITH REMARKABLE CUSTOMS—IN NORTHERN ARMENIA

celebrated throughout Russia for their superior quality, and great quantities are shipped even as far as St. Petersburg.

In the lake, at a distance of a few hundred feet from the shore, and on an island of perhaps fifty acres in extent, is located the ancient Armenian

ON THE ROAD TO LAKE SEVANGA, IN NORTHERN ARMENIA, AND ON THE ROUTE FROM ELNOFKA TO AKSTAFA

monastery of Sevanga, reputed to have been founded in the very beginning of the fourth century. At Delijan the highest point on the route is reached, at an elevation of over 7,000

DESCENT INTO THE KURA VALLEY 327

feet. From here a most excellent road sharply descends to the northward, through mountain scenery nowhere surpassed, until the little town of Akstafa is reached in the rich valley of the Kura River.

ON THE NORTHERN SLOPE OF THE LESSER CAUCASIAN MOUNTAINS, AFTER LEAVING THE DELIJAN PASS

XVI

The Caucasus—Its locality and extent—The Kura River—The Rion River—Area of the Caucasus—Population of the same—Mountain ranges—The Greater and Lesser Caucasian Mountains joined by the Suram range—Climate of Caucasia—Products of the soil—Statistics of live stock—Valleys in Eastern Caucasus—Western Caucasia—Roads—Military road from Tiflis to Vladikavkaz—Roads in Southern Caucasia and Armenia—Caucasia the gateway between Europe and Asia—Different races—Tiflis, the capital of Georgia—Its buildings, streets, etc.—The Georgian chieftain, Schemyl—The population of Tiflis—Many military and civil officials—A trip to Borjom, Abbas-Tuman, and Kutais.

WHAT is known as the Caucasus is the great isthmus, some 500 miles wide, extending east and west between the Caspian and Black seas, and joining the continents of Asia and Europe, comprising some ten or a dozen governments and provinces of Russia. Running through its centre eastward, is the Kura River, having its source in the Lesser Caucasian range of mountains on the extreme southwest part of the country. Flowing through the narrow defiles of the rugged mountains for the space of several hundred miles, its valley gradually widens beyond Tiflis until it becomes a vast level plain, forming

GENERAL VIEW OF THE CITY OF TIFLIS

AREA AND POPULATION

a border of a hundred miles or more upon the western shore of the Caspian Sea.

The Rion River runs westward, in a similar way, from the middle of the Caucasus into the Black Sea. These valleys, therefore, divide this great isthmus in an east and west direction into two sections, the northern valley formed by the Great Caucasian chain of mountains, with an average altitude of nearly 12,000 feet, and the southern one formed by the mountains of Armenia, of much less height.

The whole contains about 180,000 square miles, and has a population of quite 7,000,000. It lies, in almost equal parts, in Europe and Asia. That portion lying south of the Great Caucasian range is called the Trans-Caucasus, or Asiatic Caucasia, and it contains about five-sevenths of the whole population. The Suram range of mountains, running north and south about midway in the great isthmus, thus connects the two chains of mountains on the northern and southern borders. It is from this divide that the waterflow is eastward by the Kura River into the Caspian Sea, and to the west by the Rion River into the Black Sea.

The climate of the Caucasus is a genial one, in fact almost subtropical; snow rarely falls in the valleys or in the lower levels, although the summit of the whole majestic range of Caucasian

Mountains, owing to their great height, is perpetually covered by great masses of ice and snow.

This great height of the main chain of mountains, as well as its many branches, gives to this

STREET SCENE IN TIFLIS

country a remarkable diversity of soil, climate, and vegetable production. The mountains supply excellent pasturage for cattle and sheep, of which there are to be seen great herds everywhere. I

VIEW OF TIFLIS FROM THE FORTRESS ABOVE THE CITY

believe there are in the Caucasus over 1,000,000 horses, 6,000,000 cattle, and 15,000,000 sheep and goats.

The valleys are exceptionally fertile, and pro-

STREET SCENE IN TIFLIS

duce immense crops of wheat and other cereals. The broad valleys in the eastern part, however, have a deficient rainfall, and therefore but little of that great tract of land is cultivated. But as the

Kura River bisects it through its entire length, and would yield an ample supply of water to irrigate the entire valley, a large, and one of the most

VALLEY OF THE KURA RIVER, ABOUT ONE HUNDRED MILES EAST OF TIFLIS, AND IN THE VICINITY OF AKSTAFA

productive, regions on the globe could readily be reclaimed, which would be well suited for the culture of wheat, Indian corn, and, in fact, all the cereals, as well as grapes of unusual quality.

FLOATING WATER-MILLS ON THE KURA RIVER IN THE CITY OF TIFLIS

ROADS IN THE CAUCASUS

The western slope of the Caucasus, watered by the Rion, having ample rainfall, constitutes what is perhaps the richest tract of land in all Russia. The vegetable products of this section are unequalled in excellence and variety. Indian corn grows here and matures as perfectly as in America, and a great surplus is annually raised for export.

From the rugged and almost insurmountable nature of the Great Caucasian chain of mountains, this country has but few roads, the main one being the Georgian military road leading over the Dariel Pass, at a height of nearly 8,000 feet, from Vladikavkaz to Tiflis. There is another good road from Kutais to Vladikavkaz, and from the former city over the Lesser Caucasian range to Abbas-Tuman and Borjom. There are also the military roads running southward from Tiflis toward the northern border of Persia, via the Delijan Pass to Erivan and Djulfa, and also via Alexandropol to Kars.

With a few bridle paths, such as the famous one from Derbent on the Caspian Sea to Tiflis, one might say a fairly complete record would be given of the facilities for travel through the mountains of this rugged though picturesque country.

Having long been the gateway between Asia and Europe through which the ebb and flow of many races continued for centuries, this has naturally become a region of the most diverse ethnical characteristics. Perhaps in no other country in the world, covering so small a space, can there be found so many different races and tribes.

CAUCASIANS AND THEIR COSTUMES

While some are of the very lowest order, there are others that rank as the noblest and grandest of the human family. This is particularly true of Mingrelia and Imeritia, where perhaps the finest

FUNERAL CORTÈGE IN TIFLIS

specimens of the human race can be found. In these two provinces the women fully justify their traditional reputation for beauty, while many ex-

THE THEATRE IN TIFLIS

amples can be found among the men that are not equalled anywhere on the globe.

Tiflis has many wide, beautiful avenues and streets, well paved, and often bordered by rows of ornamental trees. There are many lines of tramways, and the streets are filled with excellent and comfortable cabs and other vehicles. It has many grand public buildings and business blocks. The palace of the governor of this province is a stately and ornate structure. A large and well-

MOUNTED COSSACKS IN PUBLIC SQUARE IN THE CITY OF TIFLIS

appointed theatre is located on one of the main avenues.

On one of the many rugged mountain heights that gird the city, the ruined battlements where the famous Georgian chieftain, Schemyl, made his last stand in defence of his country, still engage the attention of the traveller.

The Kura River, dividing the city into two nearly equal parts, and winding in a deep and sinuous gorge through it, not only provides means for excel-

A BAZAAR IN THE PERSIAN QUARTER IN THE CITY OF TIFLIS

lent drainage, but gives in many places a charming aspect to the streets and city. Being the seat of government for the Caucasus, there is a large resident military class here, as well as numerous civil officials and also many representatives of the nobility.

Resting a day or two, and visiting the many ob-

STREET SCENE IN THE PERSIAN QUARTER IN TIFLIS.

jects of interest in and about the city, I made an excursion to Borjom and Abbas-Tuman, in the Southern Caucasus. This is a region of vast parks and hunting preserves, as it is the summer home of the Grand Duke Michael, the Grand Duke George—the Crown Prince—and the Grand Duchess Xenia, together with innumerable other court satellites and dignitaries.

STREET IN THE PERSIAN QUARTER OF TIFLIS

Going over one of the wildest and most solitary passes in the world, where for safety an escort of soldiers is provided much of the way, we reached Kutais, located in one of the most fertile of valleys, where Indian corn, all the cereals, and fruits of every variety grow in the greatest luxuriance and abundance. It was the ancient Cyta, the capital of the Colchis of the Greeks, whence Jason and his freebooting band went in quest of the " Golden Fleece."

XVII

Tiflis to Mtskheta—Great antiquity of that city—Founded by near descendant of Noah—Interesting old bridge—Pompey's conquest of this country—Route over the famous Dariel Pass—Journey up the valley of the Kura River—Soil and climate of the Caucasus—Agricultural operations—Various cereals and other products—Indian corn—Primitive implements—Cattle and buffaloes used to draw the plough—Coöperative operations—Remarkable results in the production of grain in the Caucasus—The cart or arba—The new line of the Trans-Caucasian railway—Petroleum pipe line over Suram Mountains—On the road to Borjom—From Borjom to Abbas-Tuman—Over the Lesser Caucasian Mountains—Soldiers for escorts—Brigands—Magnificent view from summit—Kutais—Its history and importance—Rich valley of the Rion—Return to Tiflis.

THE railway, after leaving Tiflis, follows somewhat closely the course of the Kura River until it reaches the small town of Mtskheta. This old city is reputed to be the most ancient in all Caucasia; indeed, the local chronicler in his pride assigns it the very first place in antiquity, claiming that it is the oldest city in the world, having been founded, as is alleged, by a descendant of Noah only five generations removed. Its quaint appearance and its old churches and palaces do, indeed, stamp it as of very ancient origin, and the ruined fortresses that cover the adjacent mountains fully attest its once great strategical importance.

Near the town there is a bridge over the Kura,

GENERAL VIEW OF TIFLIS, FROM ELEVATION IN WESTERN PART OF THE CITY, LOOKING EASTWARD

in which can be found old buttresses that evidently belonged to a structure of very remote times. It is said to be a part of the bridge thrown across that river by Pompey the Great, when in pursuit of Mithridates. This powerful monarch ruled well and happily over a vast region in the East, including what is now the Caucasus, until Rome became seized with the generous desire to

ON THE KURA RIVER, IN THE WESTERN SUBURBS OF TIFLIS, ON THE ROAD TO BORJOM

include his splendid possessions within the sphere of her beneficent influence, and which finally shared the fate of that great empire when her policy of grab ultimately brought inevitable ruin.

Here the Aragya, a small river, enters the Kura from the north, after flowing through a deep, narrow, and rugged canyon. It is up the valley of this river that the military road from Tiflis to Vlad-

IN THE KURA VALLEY, BETWEEN TIFLIS AND MTSKHETA

ikavkaz runs, until it crosses the summit of the Caucasian Mountains, near Mleti, over the famous Dariel Pass, at an altitude of nearly 8,000 feet. There are many most charming bits of mountain

ON THE KURA RIVER, CAUCASIA, NEAR MTSKHETA

and landscape scenery in the neighborhood of
Mtskheta. From this place the railway continues
its western course—the valley of the Kura in the

IN THE VALLEY OF THE ARAGVA, ON THE MILITARY ROAD OVER THE
CAUCASIAN MOUNTAINS, FROM TIFLIS TO VLADIKAVKAZ

meanwhile widening into a broad, fertile plain,
until it meets the Suram range that links the
two great northern and southern chains of Caucasian Mountains together.

Pursuing my journey leisurely through this rich valley, I had the opportunity of observing somewhat the methods of agriculture practised by the natives. The soil being well adapted to the

OVER THE DARIEL PASS, ON MILITARY ROAD FROM TIFLIS TO VLADI-KAVKAZ. MOUNT KASBEK IN THE DISTANCE

culture of all cereals, and receiving an abundant rainfall, the valley lands, as also those of the first mountain slopes, are under cultivation, while in the higher regions they are used for pasture. As in the case in the Tschernozium region of Russia, to recuperate the temporary depletion of the soil

PLOUGHING IN THE KURA VALLEY

they let the lands lie fallow for the necessary period of time.

Wheat, barley, oats, and rye are the main crops, and a more or less regular rotation of them is observed. Indian corn grows well here, maturing in the most perfect manner, and constitutes the main cereal food of the inhabitants of the Western Caucasus. In cases where there is a scarcity of land, Indian corn is planted immediately after the wheat or barley crop has been gathered. The insufficient time thus allotted, however, does not permit it always to mature, in which event it is secured and used as a green fodder for cattle.

The implements are of the crudest and most primitive character. The plough employed to break up the land is a large, unwieldy affair, and evidently constructed by the farmer himself. It has a wooden mould-board, and is in fact almost wholly made of wood. It, however, turns a wide and, what is more to the purpose, a very deep furrow, as from three to eight pairs of oxen or buffaloes are used to draw it. Only the Russians use horses for ploughing in the Caucasus.

They have a curious sort of coöperative association of farmers here, its object being to facilitate and cheapen farming operations. One member who does not possess a team will furnish the plough; another who has no plough will supply the team; the third and fourth will either act as ploughmen or supply some requisite not possessed by the others. By this joint arrangement the lands of the association are ploughed, when the company

SCENE IN A FARM VILLAGE ON THE ARAGVA

is dissolved, after a continuance of a fortnight or three weeks.

Equally crude appliances are employed to harrow the land, and otherwise put it in condition to receive the seed, and which generally is in wonderful tilth when the primitive means used are considered. Indeed, the great yield of grains by

SCENE BETWEEN MIKHAILOV AND BORJOM

such simple means and at such small cost inclines one to inquire whether, after all, an adequate increase would follow the use of more perfect implements and a more up-to-date system of farming.

CART, OR ARBA, USED FOR FARM AND ROAD PURPOSES

Certainly, the results in the Caucasus are not to be despised, for there is produced each year in that country, above home requirements, more than one hundred millions of bushels of grain available for export to foreign countries, or about fifteen bushels per capita—a result not equalled by any other country.

A curious vehicle is used for farm purposes, called the arba. It is a cart the wheels of which are of extraordinary size, and usually fixed rigidly to the axle, thus rotating with it instead of each having an independent movement. At Mikhailov a road branches to the southwest, following up the valley of the Kura as far as Borjom. This road is to be extended over the Lesser Caucasian range of mountains, toward Kars and Erzeroum.

The main line of this, the Trans-Caucasian, railroad continues westward, crossing the Suram Mountains at an elevation of nearly 6,000 feet. The engineering difficulties encountered in this portion of the route were very great, and the road reflects credit upon both the energy and skill of those who executed it. At the summit, the road passes through a tunnel of some two and one-half miles in length. As this line is extensively used to transport petroleum from Baku to Batoum, on the Black Sea, important arrangements are being made to pump the oil over this high range of mountains, and thus avoid the expense and difficulty which now attend its carriage by rail. Already great tanks and pumping stations are being

VIEW NEAR GORI, ON THE KURA RIVER

constructed at Mikhailov for this purpose, and large pipes have been laid to the summit, a distance of some thirty miles. As the summit is between 6,000 and 7,000 feet above the Black Sea,

IN THE KURA VALLEY

the petroleum will be conducted thence in pipes to Batoum, and, flowing freely by its own gravity, it will save the cost of nearly 150 miles of transportation by rail.

Borjom is a charming summer resort, nestled

among picturesque mountains and along the banks of the Kura River, whose rapid current pours in swift torrents from the mountain gorges above. Very celebrated mineral springs are located here,

PERSIAN MINISTER'S RESIDENCE IN BORJOM

the waters of which are shipped to all parts of the empire. Many splendid villas and residences are scattered throughout this romantic region. The palace of his Imperial Highness the Grand Duke

Michael is beautifully located on the banks of the river, some distance above the city. I was especially interested in a most artistic and ornate dwelling occupied by the Persian minister, who resides here.

A most excellent road runs from Borjom to Abbas-Tuman, a distance of about sixty miles. As

THE SUMMER PALACE OF HIS IMPERIAL HIGHNESS THE GRAND DUKE MICHAEL, ON THE BANKS OF THE KURA RIVER, NEAR BORJOM

relays are provided at intervals of twelve miles, a dash through this lovely country is most charming. At Abbas-Tuman, the Crown Prince George— second son of the late Czar—has a rustic palace embowered in the groves of a beautiful park. From Abbas-Tuman to Kutais is a distance of nearly eighty miles, which is usually driven in a day. The road to the summit leads up the steep slope of the mountain, through a wild and dreary region. These mountain passes are still infested with many brigands, and many thrilling stories are told of their terrible doings, even in spite of all the precautions of the government.

HIS IMPERIAL HIGHNESS GRAND DUKE MICHAEL ON HIS DAILY DRIVE IN BORJOM

For the safety of the inhabitants and travellers, the whole country is protected by Cossacks, and all along the road there are soldiers stationed at intervals of a few versts. When a carriage passes, several soldiers follow until they are released by the next squad. They increase in number as the

MARKET SCENE IN KUTAIS

ESCORT OF SOLDIERS

summit is approached, where, when reached, there are usually ten or a dozen soldiers as escorts. It is beyond words to describe the grandeur of the panorama that suddenly bursts upon the view

SOLDIER ON THE MOUNTAIN SIDE, AFTER LEAVING ABBAS-TUMAN, ON THE ROAD TO KUTAIS, OVER THE LESSER CAUCASIAN MOUNTAINS

as the summit is attained, which is done most abruptly.

The stately chain of Caucasian Mountains stretches before you, extending several hundred miles to the northwest. As they are nearly 100 miles distant, and viewed across the broad valley of the Rion, an immense section of this great range can be seen, which is snow-capped throughout almost its whole length. Projecting above the

STREET SCENE IN KUTAIS

common summit-level are the ice-tipped peaks of the Elbruz, away off in the distance, to the left, and rising to a height of 18,500 feet; of Ikhara, Koshtan Tau, and Dych Tau, over 17,000 feet in height; and finally, far to the right, the symmetrical Kazbek, rising 16,500 feet above the sea.

ON THE SUMMIT OF THE LESSER CAUCASIAN MOUNTAINS. RUSSIAN AND COSSACK GUARDS

BEAUTIFUL MOUNTAIN VIEW 377

Thus a stretch of fully 300 miles of this grand range of mountains lies before you, clothed, for much of its height, in a mantle of snow.

A rapid drive of seven hours brings us to the

MARKET SCENE IN KUTAIS.

important city of Kutais, the capital of the province of that name. It is on the Rion, or, as the Greeks called it, the Phasis River. It was from this name that the word "pheasant" was derived, as this fowl was once in great abundance in the mountains at the head-waters of the Phasis River. Kutais lies in the midst of one of the richest countries in the world, where all vegetation grows profusely. It is said that almost all kinds of fruits, even apples, pears, apricots, etc., grow abundantly in a wild state in the neighboring forests. In view of the richness of this country, it is no wonder that the covetous Greek was tempted to leave his barren shores to seek the golden fleece in this highly favored land.

Kutais has many interesting and attractive markets and bazaars, at which curious and beautiful fabrics in silk and wool are sold. There is a school here of much importance, designed especially for instruction in horticulture. Kutais has one of the finest examples of Georgian architecture, in a church erected in the eleventh century. Tempted by its wealth, the city has been plundered and destroyed again and again by the Persians, Mongolians, Turks, and other invading races.

XVIII

Return to Tiflis—Special permit to visit Central Asia—Great courtesy of the American Ambassador, Hon. E. A. Hitchcock—Return to Baku—Passage across the Caspian Sea—Arrival at Krasnovodsk—A look about that city—Rapid growth of same—Its harbor and other natural advantages—Will become an important city—Railway station—Splendid structure—Curious mixture of natural products—Blending of Oriental and Occidental races—Possible result—Russia's fondness for American products—Use of same in Russia—Her probable future demand for Western products—America's opportunity—Trains on the Trans-Caspian railway—Courtesy of the railway officials—Emigrants to the far East—Departure from Krasnovodsk—New petroleum field—Minerals and metals here—Uzum-Ada, the old terminus of railway—The plains of Turcomania—Persian Mountains—Central Asia—A vast depressed basin—Caspian Sea below ocean level—Similar depression in Sahara Desert—Russia's Central Asian possessions—Sterility of Turcomania due to lack of rainfall—Oasis of Merv—Strabo's reference to it—Three great level plateaus—Amu-Daria and Syr-Daria Rivers.

On returning to Tiflis, the ever-present desire of visiting Central Asia again possessing me, my guide suggested that I call upon Prince Gallatzin, the Governor-General of the Caucasus, who might possibly issue the necessary permit. As was the case at Baku, this functionary informed me that he had no authority to issue one, and that it could be obtained only by direct application to the Ministry at St. Petersburg. In order to save time, he, however, advised me to communicate by telegraph with the United States Ambassador at that city, feeling assured that by his intervention a permit would be readily secured. This I accordingly did.

Through the great courtesy and prompt application of our most efficient Ambassador there, the Hon. E. A. Hitchcock, in a wonderfully short space of time I received a long telegram direct from the Russian Minister of the Interior, giving the desired permit, with the information, also, that he had telegraphed instructions to the Governor of East Caucasus at Baku, to the Governor of Turcomania at Merv, the military agent at Bokhara, and the Governor of Turkestan at Samarkand and Tashkent. Armed with this magic "open sesame," I at once set out on my journey. Before going, however, I took the precaution to employ an additional guide, who was familiar with the various languages of that country of mixed tongues.

On arriving at Baku, I found that the governor had already called upon the proprietor of the hotel, and had left instructions to be informed of our arrival. He received us with every mark of civility and courtesy, and arranged for our departure on the boat that evening. He also detailed the police agent of the city to wait upon us, which enabled me to see many things in this curious city that I was unable to see on my former visit.

Our passage across the Caspian Sea naturally was a boisterous one, since it is numbered among the most tempestuous waters. Being fringed on most of its western and southern borders by two mountain ranges, among the highest on the globe, and its eastern shore forming the western verge of the hot, arid plains of Turcomania, such conditions of extreme heat and cold here exist as are likely to result in the sudden development of violent gales.

Arriving at Krasnovodsk in the morning, we found that the train for the east did not leave until the evening. This gave us an opportunity of looking about this new city, the recently established terminus of this great railway.

Uzum-Ada, about sixty miles to the southeast, on the bay of that name, was formerly the terminus of the railway. On account of the excellent harbor, the fact that it shortens the sea route by nearly seventy miles, and other advantages, the present location was selected about three years ago. Up to that time, it was an obscure Tartar fishing village. It is now a busy, thriving town of nearly 10,000 inhabitants, with wide streets, excellent public and private buildings, electric lights, etc.

A low, rocky, and sterile range of mountains,

KRASNOVODSK AND HARBOR, THE WESTERN TERMINUS OF THE TRANS-CASPIAN RAILWAY, ON THE EASTERN SHORE OF THE CASPIAN SEA

sweeping from the shore in a semicircular course, encloses a space like a large amphitheatre, whereon the city is built. The railway station here is a rare gem of architecture. It is entirely of hewn stone, and merges in its composition the choicest elements of Eastern art. It is a splendid composite of Persian, Saracenic, and Central Asian, with even a tinge of Chinese and Hindu. The station, like most of those at the main towns of this line, has a very large and high central room used as a combined waiting and dining room, while at either end of the building are located the various apartments used for the purposes of the company.

In this zone, where the East and the West overlap in such a bewildering manner, some strange affiliations occur. In the main room, with its exquisite Mohammedan doors and windows, can be seen depending from a splendid ceiling of the purest arabesque and decorated in the most enchanting colors, a huge Venetian chandelier, holding incandescent electric lights, made in Austria, and supplied with a current from an engine and dynamo built in Germany. In the middle of the room is a large and elegantly carved table from France and chairs from Italy, while in one corner of the room, for the purpose of weighing luggage, is a splendid American platform scale made in Vermont.

Such a medley of arts and confusion of races lead to some strange reflections. The rapidly growing conflict between and the ever-increasing tendency toward a blending of things Occidental and Oriental, suggest a possible ultimate fusion, out of which there may arise a neutral state of races wherein the softening idealism of the East

NEW RAILWAY STATION AT KRASNOVODSK, THE WESTERN TERMINUS OF THE TRANS-CASPIAN RAILWAY

will give a soul to the inflexible materiality of the West, which in return will impart a substance to Oriental dreams and abstractions.

In my travels throughout this great empire, it was impossible for me not to observe everywhere the many evidences of Russian fondness, and even partiality for, American products, especially machinery. Even the locomotive that drew the train over the first section of the Trans-Siberian railway, and also that used on the Trans-Caspian railway to Askabad, were American, built in Philadelphia.

On the Siberian route it is no uncommon thing to see, at the stations, American agricultural machinery destined to be used in those regions. At one station I saw a freight train in which there was a car loaded with mining machinery and machinists' tools, the product of American workshops.

Considering the immense population of this country, its long and steadfast friendship for America, and the still further fact that in order to develop her own incalculable resources and those of the other Asiatic nations into which she is carrying her influence, there must be created wants far in excess of her own ability to supply, thus necessitating extensive purchases from other nations, it seems evident that, by a proper effort on our part, this, of all countries in the world, could become the most important and profitable field for American enterprise. If, unfortunately, we should neglect to avail ourselves of the full advantages of a situation so promising, I trust at least that we will not suffer ourselves to be decoyed into an attitude of hostility to Russia, with no better result than to play into the hands of some ambitious and selfish nation.

There are trains leaving daily for the East on the Trans-Caspian railway, but as they are mixed freight and passenger trains, designed to carry soldiers, emigrants, merchandize, and material for new railways under construction farther on, they offer no facilities or comforts for the traveller. There is, however, a train that leaves here three times a week, consisting wholly of second, third, and fourth class passenger cars, for the purpose of accommodating the better class of travel, which is rapidly on the increase. This train, usually composed of twelve or fifteen cars, presents a neat and pleasing appearance, all the cars being painted snow white, even to the locomotive. They are plain in the interior, with uncovered seats, and but little comfort. Those who design travelling at night are obliged to provide themselves, before starting, with bedding, linen, towels, etc. As I have before stated, this line being a military road, all the officials of the train, the engineer, the fireman, and even the workmen on the track, are drawn from the army.

On presenting my passport and telegram to the proper official, he at once, with the utmost polite-

TRANS-CASPIAN RAILWAY TRAIN

ness, conducted me to the train and assigned me a whole compartment. While the train was being made up, I noticed that a large number of emigrants were embarking on it.

On inquiry I was informed that it was a group of over 100 families, which the government was assisting to emigrate from the overcrowded and at present unfortunate district of Saratov, on the Volga. As indicating the paternal policy of the government, as well as the growing efflux of people from the older into the newer provinces of the empire, I would say that they were bound for the extreme eastern part of Turkestan, 150 miles beyond Tashkent, and that the government was granting fifty to eighty acres of land to each adult, besides 100 rubles to each family.

On leaving Krasnovodsk, the train for a short space runs directly eastward, when it bears south, running for a distance of twenty or thirty miles along the shore of the Caspian Sea, and at the foot of the low, rugged range of mountains that dip sharply into its waters. At a distance of about five miles, the road crosses at a low level a somewhat extensive peninsula, upon which I noticed a number of what seemed to be new oil wells. I was told that recent explorations disclose important petroleum deposits in these regions, and that there are now in operation some twenty wells, with many new ones being sunk. It is said that already there is enough produced here to meet the present wants of this side of the Caspian,

NEW OIL WELLS RECENTLY OPENED ON THE SHORES OF THE CASPIAN SEA, ON THE LINE OF RAILWAY BELOW KRASNOVODSK

with every prospect of an ample surplus for export at an early day.

It might be added that the hills and mountains in this vicinity abound in iron, copper, salt, sulphur, graphite, and other minerals that must ulti-

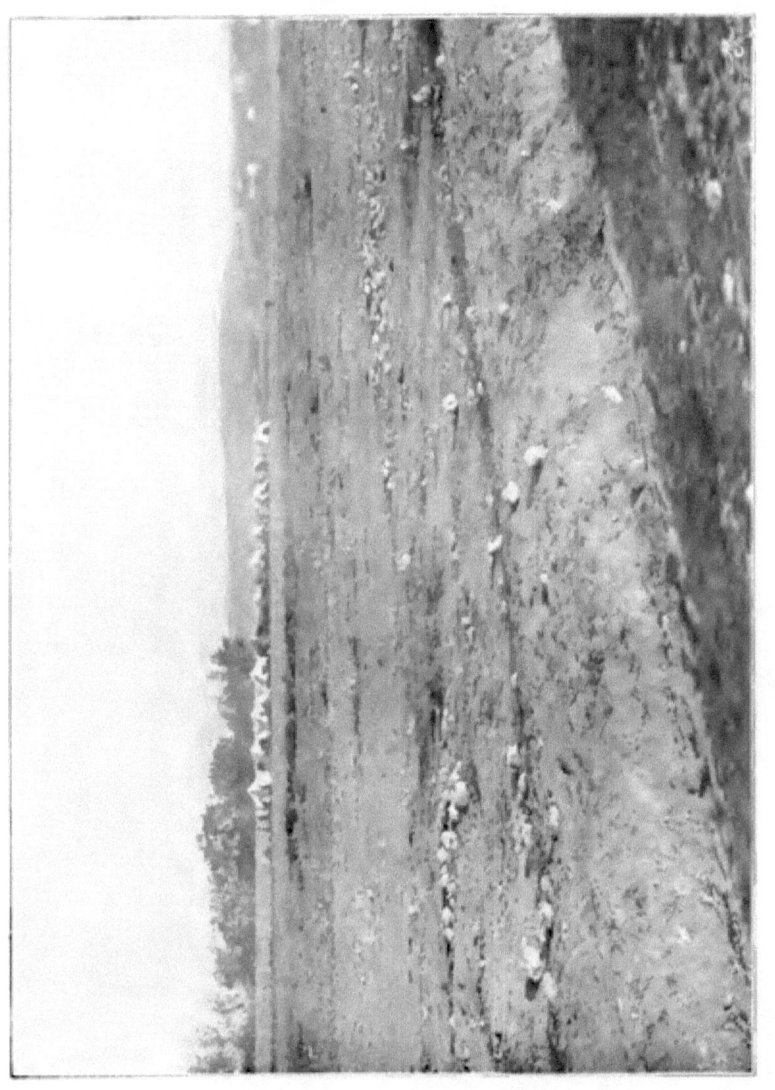

RUSSIAN MILITARY ENCAMPMENT ON OPEN PLAINS

GREAT CENTRAL BASIN

mately be a resource of great value to the vast and purely agricultural regions eastward.

On leaving Uzum-Ada, the original terminus of the line, the railway takes a due southern course and enters at once upon the arid plains of Turcomania that, like a great sheet of water, stretch north and south through a distance of nearly 700 miles, at a height of nearly 200 feet above the sea. As the low range of mountains cutting from the Caspian eastward into the desert slowly recedes from the sight, there comes as gradually into view the lofty mountains that rise like a mighty rampart from the plains of Turcomania, and running for 400 miles along the northern border of Persia.

Central Asia presents some remarkable geological and physical characteristics. In a somewhat irregular form, and covering an area of nearly 1,500,000 square miles, it constitutes a great depressed basin, even descending—as in the case of the Caspian Sea, with an area of nearly 200,000 square miles—to some depth below the level of the ocean. Into this great basin, the Volga, Ural, and Emba rivers from the north; the Atok, Murgab, Amu-Daria, Syr-Daria, and many other streams from the south and east, pour their mighty floods chiefly into the Caspian and Aral seas, which, for the want of a channel to the ocean, find their only outlet by evaporation.

A similar depression exists in Africa, with the difference that it is smaller in extent, and that there are no large rivers discharging into it. While at Chott-Melgig, in the northern Sahara, some years ago, I was informed that the shallow salt lake

STATION ON TRANS-CASPIAN RAILWAY

there lay some hundreds of feet below the level of the Mediterranean, and that if the waters of that sea were conducted into it by a canal—regarded by engineers as practicable—a large interior sea would be formed.

What is known as Russia's Central Asian possessions, containing nearly 1,500,000 square miles, are made up of the provinces of Turcomania, Bokhara, and Khiva—still semi-independent khanates—Turkestan, and the important though somewhat indefinite territory recently acquired in Ferghan and the Pamirs, near the northwest border of India.

Turcomania is, throughout, an almost level plain, extending from the northern border of Afghanistan in a northwestern direction about 800 miles, and with a width of 300 or 400 miles. A great portion of it is almost destitute of vegetation, excepting a sort of dry tufted grass, the natural product of an arid soil, and in which the camel finds a fairly nutritious food. The sterility of this country is almost wholly due to the lack of rainfall, as its soil possesses great natural fertility, being no doubt, throughout much of its extent, the deposit in primeval times of those great rivers now running into the Aral Sea, and which once, as is very probable, found their way into the Caspian Sea.

All along its western border, skirted by the Persian mountains, which send down many streams that are used for irrigation, there is a broad zone of wonderfully productive land reaching far into the plain, a test of what a great part of this country might become with an adequate supply of water. Remote as this may seem, it is not among the impossibilities, as the great Amu-Daria, running along and near the eastern border of Turcomania, is of a sufficient elevation to permit its

VIEW ACROSS THE PLAINS OF TURCOMANIA, BETWEEN ASKABAD AND DUSHAK, ON THE TRANS-CASPIAN RAILWAY

waters being carried and distributed through the greater part of the plain below.

The oasis of Merv—the southeastern portion of this province, and watered by the Murgab River, having its source in the Afghan mountains—is little inferior in size, and in its marvellous fertility and wonderful productiveness is quite equal, to the Nile valley. Strabo, in referring to this region, says that the vines sometimes grew so large that two men with outstretched arms could scarcely circle them, and that bunches of grapes were produced two cubits in length.

By a rather easy ascent, the level plateau of Bokhara is reached, a country of about 150,000 square miles area, unsurpassed for the richness of its soil and the variety and exuberance of its products. Through another incline is reached the last plateau of Turkestan, which stretches away to the foot-hills of the Altai Mountains and to the southern border of Siberia.

Russia's Central Asian possessions may therefore be roughly described as consisting of three great level plateaus, rising in successive steps one above the other, and extending from the Caspian Sea in the west to the western border of China in the east. The Syr-Daria traverses the lower border of Turkestan, the waters of which it is possible to turn into the khanates of Bokhara and Khiva. As in like manner the Amu-Daria runs along the lower border of Khiva and Bokhara, its waters might similarly be turned into Turcomania, which would make these countries among the richest and most productive on the globe.

A somewhat similar distribution of these waters must have existed in former times, converting into fertile plains great areas of what are now waste, uncultivated lands. This alone can account for the presence of those immense multitudes that once peopled these regions, the evidence of which one discovers on all hands.

XIX

The old bed of the Amu-Daria River—Across a desert—Oasis of Kizyl-Arvat—Among the Turcomanians—A splendid race—His dwelling—Women in Turcomania—Custom of polygamy—Purchase of wives—Weaving of rugs and carpets—Their crude device for same—Work done mainly by girls—Inferiority of the new to the old product—Wealth of the Turcoman—Their food, clothing, etc.—The camel—Roads in Turcomania—Caravans of camels—Along the Persian border—Askabad—New and beautiful city—Vegetable products of this region—Culture of cotton—Old Teke towns.

THE railway, after leaving the Caspian Sea, for a space of fifty or sixty miles follows a well-defined ancient river-bed, considered by scientists to be that of the mighty Amu-Daria, of which some engineers claim to have discovered a fairly traceable channel from Kerki, running due west and entering the Caspian Sea at a point near where the railway leaves the shore. For nearly 150 miles the railway crosses a true desert, destitute alike of vegetation and water, the latter having to be hauled for the purposes of the road and for domestic uses along the entire section from Kizyl-Arvat, a point where the line touches the Kuran-Dagh, a spur of the Kopet-Dagh or Persian Mountains, and where fresh water is first obtained. A perennial stream of water here, descending from the mountains and used for irrigation, has created an oasis of considerable size, the

TURCOMANIAN TARTARS AT KIZYL-ARVAT STATION ON THE TRANS-CASPIAN RAILWAY

vegetal wealth and beauty of which was in most agreeable contrast with the sterile country through which we passed.

TURCOMANIANS AND THEIR YURTS OR TENTS

Here we find ourselves in the midst of the Turcoman Tartars, whose dreary and solitary domain extends indefinitely to the west and north. This is physically by far the most splendid race I

TURCOMAN VILLAGE ON THE PLAINS OF TURCOMANIA, BETWEEN KIZYL-ARVAT AND ASKABAD.

have ever seen. They are, without exception, unusually tall, much above the medium, and it is rare to meet with one of ordinary stature. Even men of advanced age walk with a step so elastic and in a manner so erect as to excite wonder. They possess an open and often a pleasing countenance, regular features, and almost always a piercing and beautiful eye. Like the Kirghiz, they live in tents. Unlike that race, however, who ordinarily cluster their tents into villages, the Turcoman scatters his at wider intervals throughout the country he occupies. The admirable physical and other traits of this people are no doubt the outgrowth of the open, independent life they have so long lived.

The tent of the Turcoman is round, usually from fifteen to thirty feet in diameter, and in its exterior aspect is anything but attractive, being often weather-worn and dingy. In passing into it, no change can be more startling. It is like the rapid shifting of a scene in a theatre, so sudden is the transformation. It is difficult to conceive anything more exquisite than the interior one often sees in the tent of a well-to-do Turcoman. The floor is covered with carpets and rugs of charming designs and exquisite coloring. The walls are encircled with lovely hangings and tapestries, and the door shielded by portières of richest design, all of which is the handiwork of this singular race.

The women do not, as is so often the case with the men, carry into their advancing years the remnants of the grace and beauty that marked the vigorous period of their life. They are, moreover, only of medium stature. The girls, as a rule, have only ordinary attractions, but some-

TURCOMAN TENTS

times are distinctly beautiful. They literally bespangle themselves with gold and silver ornaments, coins, etc., and they display rings of turquoise, and such other jewels as they can command. Their costume is of graceful design, richly embroidered, and of enchanting coloring, the invariable product of their own fair hands.

TURCOMAN TARTARS AT GEOK-TEPE, STATION ON THE TRANS-CASPIAN RAILWAY

Polygamy is still prevalent among them, as is also the custom of purchasing their wives. A father is esteemed fortunate who has a large family of daughters, as they are sure to bring him a rich reward, the more comely selling for from 500 to 800 and even 1,000 rubles. The father who has an equal number of daughters and sons applies the money obtained by the disposal of his daughters to the purchase of wives for his sons. He is distinctly the lord and master of his household, and their habits and customs often discover the ancient patriarchal traces of the Eastern races.

Being anxious to see how the beautiful carpets and rugs were produced, which connoisseurs here now esteem as the richest product of Eastern textile art, I visited quite a number of their homes for that purpose. The smaller ones are woven in the tents occupied by the family, but for the larger ones a temporary canopy is erected near by. The ground is covered by some old carpet or other protection for the future fabric. Two poles, of a length suited to the width of the carpet to be made, are placed at a distance apart to correspond with its length. From one pole to the other the warp is extended and spaced to suit the fineness of the carpet. The warp is made taut by twisting one of the poles, which are securely staked to the ground to prevent them being drawn together, and to preserve the necessary tightness. As the only remaining bit of mechanism is a heavy metallic comb used from time to time to drive the pile firmly together, it will be seen that the rude simplicity of their appliances is only equalled by the marvellous results produced by it.

The work is done almost wholly by women, and most generally by young girls. They are seated

TURCOMAN GIRLS WEAVING CARPETS UNDER A TEMPORARY CANOPY ADJOINING THEIR TENT

on the ground in a row, each girl having before her a number of woollen balls of the various colors required by the proposed designs of the carpet. A short length or tuft of the woollen thread is dexterously entwined between several threads of the warp, and secured by a loop which is cut off at a length about double that which the pile is

TURCOMAN TENT ON THE PLAINS OF TARTARY

intended to be when finished. After several courses are completed, the pile is driven together by the metallic comb, and is then clipped off with great care and skill to the proper length. The most astounding thing in the whole process is that no pattern whatever is used, the women relying wholly upon their memory and the eye for the arrangement of the colors and development of the pattern and designs. As, in the case of very fine examples, scarcely more than twenty to thirty square inches can be completed by a single operative in a day, some of the larger carpets require an incredibly long time for completion. I was shown one of moderate size, on which three girls had been working for over four months, which was not yet three-fourths done. It is said that several girls join together and purchase the necessary material, sharing in the end jointly the proceeds of their united labor.

It is at once apparent to any one at all versed in this art that the modern product is vastly inferior to that of the olden time. They themselves are fully aware of this, for when displaying a sample, if you ask them if it is an antique, they at once ruefully shake their heads, as if regretting to confess that they no longer create those miracles of texture and color of their ancestors. It is well nigh impossible to obtain superior examples of the old work even here, so thoroughly have the Persian, Armenian, and other merchants searched the country, and, when found, exorbitant prices are asked and paid.

CAMEL CARAVAN CROSSING THE PLAINS OF TURCOMANIA

Almost the entire wealth and resources of the Turcomans are comprised in their herds and flocks, as they disdain to cultivate the soil. They raise few cattle, but have immense herds of sheep and goats. It is upon their sheep that they rely mainly for their food and the material for their clothing. They usually wear a coat or cloak, called a khalat, made from the skin of that animal, and a huge cap made of the pelt of the same animal.

They have, besides, great numbers of camels. This is the true home of that patient and useful creature, and I cannot remember ever having seen so many in any country. It is his constant companion, using it to carry his burdens, even hitching it to his rude cart, or to his still ruder plough, should he so far forget the traditions of his ancestors as to use so plebeian an implement.

The Turcoman possesses, also, a famous breed of horses, which, although not desirable in appearance, are noted for their powers of endurance, being capable of performing long and trying journeys. It is reported that they can go from fifty to sixty miles for days in succession, and that also with but little food. They are long of back, neck, and limb, and have a scant coat of fine hair, but their highly useful qualities compensate for their lack of beauty.

There are few, if any, common roads for vehicles

in Turcomania; but cutting in various directions through the treeless and almost trackless waste are camel trails, on which, under a cloudless sky

VIEW ACROSS THE DESERT OF TURCOMANIA, LOOKING TOWARD THE PERSIAN MOUNTAINS

and over burning sands, can be seen long caravans of camels plodding their drowsy, solemn way to distant lands beyond, with which they hold a rude, though not unimportant, commerce.

ALONG THE BORDER OF PERSIA 415

From Kizyl-Arvat, for more than 300 miles, the railway line closely hugs the base of the mountain range that forms the boundary line between Tur-

TURCOMAN VILLAGE ON THE OPEN PLAINS, BETWEEN GEOK-TEPE AND ASKABAD

comania and Persia, and the train is therefore seldom more than a few miles from the border of the latter country. This may, perhaps, have a significance in the future relations of these two nations.

416   SIBERIA AND CENTRAL ASIA

Askabad, located about midway between Krasnovodsk and Merv, is a beautiful town of considerable size, having something like 25,000 or 30,000 inhabitants. It has been entirely built up since Russia first occupied this country, scarcely twelve

STATION AT ASKABAD, ON TRANS-CASPIAN RAILWAY

years ago; its population is composed almost wholly of Russians, mostly army officials, soldiers, and the large class of industrious people who follow in the wake of the army, and who permanently identify themselves with the interests and

CITY OF ASKABAD

fortunes of the new countries acquired. Like all new Russian towns in these regions, it has wide, well-paved streets, and beautiful avenues of trees, with a stream of running water on either side of

STATION OF DJU-DJU-KLY, ON THE TRANS-CASPIAN RAILWAY

the streets. Having an abundance of water, supplied by a stream descending from the adjacent mountains, most of which is used for irrigation, Askabad has become the centre of a large and highly productive agricultural region.

SCENE NEAR ASKABAD

ing grown in considerable quantities. The quality is fairly good, and the yield very heavy; both, no doubt, being capable of much improvement in the future, as at present it is being grown by the un-

IRRIGATING CANALS IN OASIS OF MERV

skilled labor of the Turcoman and the immigrant Russian, who have as yet but little knowledge of this peculiar plant.

The city is located some miles away from the old Teke town, which was once of great importance, being formerly one of many defences established by the Tartars against Russian encroachment.

XX

Location of towns on Russian railways—Her occupation of new countries—Dushak, the southern point of the road—Irrigation of oasis of Merv—New city of Merv—Railway from Merv to Herat—Confidence of Russia in Central Asia—Growth of cotton—The ancient city of Merv—Extraordinary mounds—Home of Kuldja Khan—Curious custom of naming women—Fertility of the oasis of Merv—Pasture land and jungles—Wild animals—In the old city of Merv—Its extent and history—Complete desolation—Home of wild beasts—Former population—Founded by Alexander the Great—Its destruction.

It is in order here to refer to a practice of the government in locating the stations of its railways, so general as to indicate a fixed policy. In extending its railway lines through the countries it occupies, the stations of the road are invariably located at some distance, and often many miles, away from the native towns in the region through which they pass. Thus the new, or railway, town of Merv is twenty-five miles from the old city of that name; the new, or Russian, Bokhara is twelve miles from the old city; and the station of new Samarkand from four to five miles away from the ancient city. In occupying old countries, it seems to be the purpose of the government to soften the

EXTRAORDINARY MOUNDS NEAR MERV

collision of the new with the older order of things, relying on the truly Oriental process of slow absorption, rather than the more modern one of pressure and compulsion.

It seems to be her policy to allow the older communities and cities the fullest possible freedom to enjoy and exercise their ancient rights, customs, and habits; and to this end she seeks to avoid those violent shocks, changes, and disturbances that must inevitably result from bringing into an unduly near position the influences of a new and too often incongruous civilization. By this precaution the two will ultimately, insensibly, and peacefully merge, the one by gradual decline, and the other through a steady advance.

At Dushak, the road reaches its extreme southern point, whence it takes a northeastern course to Merv. The intermediate country is well cultivated, a condition rendered possible by the waters of the Tedjen River, flowing northward, and the irrigating Alikhanof Canal, that taps the Murgab River at some distance above Merv.

This town has grown with great rapidity the past few years, having now from 15,000 to 20,000 inhabitants. Being most favorably located for strategic and commercial purposes, it is destined to some day become a city of much importance.

From here a railway is being built southward

and up the Murgab River, and is already completed almost to the very Afghan border. To insure its early completion, the government, for some reason, has recently been pushing it with much vigor, working upon it both night and day. It is

HOME OF KULDJA KHAN

also hinted that Russia is quietly, though rapidly, extending the line to Herat, the key to Northern Afghanistan.

I was received with great courtesy by the military agent here, through whose kindness I was enabled to see the various objects in and about

DISTANT VIEW OF OLD CITY OF MERV

GATEWAY INTO OLD CITY OF MERV

the city. Like all the new Russian towns, the city is laid out with great regularity, the streets running at right angles and fringed on both sides with rows of beautiful trees. The private residences are elegant, with all the modern improvements, and almost always located in the middle of a great square, forming a splendid park. A handsome boulevard of several miles in length, and ornamented by a double row of trees on either side, extends through the city. Owing to the richness of the soil, bright sunshine, and abundance of water for irrigation, the creation of a beautiful park or delightful boulevard in this genial climate is the work of only a few years.

From the extent and solidity of the improvements seen everywhere, the Russian has evidently entered this country with great confidence, and to stay.

Unlike some nations, she does not send to her newly acquired possessions a favored class only, to enjoy the emoluments of office or the dignity of administering their civil and political affairs; but, regarding each new possession as the property of the whole nation, she hastens to people it with her industrial classes, who engage in every branch of trade and agriculture.

In Merv, as in all new towns in this country, the Russian element vastly predominates. There are large and excellently appointed barracks here, and there are many soldiers, it being an important military centre.

Cotton is extensively grown in this oasis, as also in Bokhara, and in the district of Ferghan further eastward. In all of these provinces, such reports are in circulation regarding the marvellous yield secured as to at least indicate that this is to become an industry of the highest importance in Central Asia.

As I have stated, the ancient city of Merv—or, rather, what was once the ancient city, as it is now merely a mass of crumbling ruins—is located some twenty-five miles from the new town built on the railway line. Although there is a station at Bairom-Ali, not far from the ruins, I preferred to drive thither over a tolerable road, since it afforded me an opportunity to observe the habits of the natives, and to study at short range the more important features of the country.

About midway there looms up a series of wonderful mounds, the extraordinary size of which, suggesting an incredible amount of labor to create, entitles them to be classed among the greatest of curiosities. At a distance they look like a low range of mountains, or, rather, very high hills. They are right in the centre of a great level plain. My inquiries as to their origin and purpose

IN THE OLD CITY OF MERV

elicited no other information than that they were probably in some way related to Alexander's conquest and occupation of this country. Their

IN THE OLD CITY OF MERV

obvious military character and evident antiquity lend some support to this theory.

A few miles further on, delightfully nestled in a beautiful grove, is a handsome white structure of the purest Oriental type. It is said to be the palace of the princess by whose treaty the Russians came into possession of this country, some ten or twelve years ago. She is the widow of the last reigning Khan of Turcomania, and is called by the Tartars Kuldja Khan, which literally means the "flower of the khan."

These people have a singular though truly chivalrous custom of naming their women, the name being usually that of a flower, its color, or some feature of it.

Along the whole route I found the land to be of surpassing fertility, and the country literally gridironed by canals and ditches for the purpose of irrigation. Being the property of the Tartars, who do not cultivate the soil, depending mainly on pasturage, it is covered with a heavy growth of grass, which at times, uniting with a dense mass of shrubbery, forms throughout great areas an impenetrable jungle.

Wild animals, therefore, of almost every variety, even to the tiger, find here a secure home. Our driver informed us that only a day or two before, some soldiers killed a fine specimen of this animal that was found prowling uncomfortably near their quarters.

We enter the old town through an immense archway in the middle of a long, massive, though half-

WALLS AND GATEWAY OF THE OLD CITY OF MERV

decayed wall, that formed one of the many ramparts of this once mighty city. It baffles the imagination to conceive, or the tongue to describe, the wide prospect of ruin and desolation that spreads before the view. Extending in all directions as far as the eye can reach, there is nothing

DISTANT VIEW OF MERV

but great heaps of rubbish, crumbling walls and buildings, broken arches, with here and there the half-preserved ruins of some majestic edifice towering over all, and standing like a solemn, solitary sentinel to guard the sad remains of former splendor and greatness.

440 SIBERIA AND CENTRAL ASIA

RUINED MOSQUE OF THE SULTAN SANJARE

Not a single human creature now dwells in this silent city; the ghoulish hyena and noisy jackal find their lair in what was once the glory and home

RUINED MOSQUE IN OLD CITY OF MERV

of nearly 2,000,000 people. The guide, observing our astonishment, requested us to turn our glass toward an object faintly visible in the distant horizon. "That," said he, "is the mosque of the Sultan Sanjare; it is nearly six miles away, and directly in the centre of the ruined city."

The ruins of many mosques, palaces, and other buildings, some yet rising to the height of several hundred feet, are sufficiently well preserved to enable one to form some idea of what must have been the beauty and grandeur of these stately structures. Many streets are sufficiently intact to indicate the former bustle, throng, and traffic of its great thoroughfares.

It is somewhat difficult to fix with any degree of precision the limits of the ancient city. It is, however, evident that it must at some time have covered a space of from thirty to forty miles in circumference, or an area quite as great as that of New York or Paris.

Its greatest former population is variously estimated at 1,500,000 to 2,000,000. The extraordinary territory covered may be somewhat accounted for by the fact that in past time it was the custom—one that has, in a large measure, survived in Oriental countries—for the better classes to surround their houses with large gardens and parks, enclosed within the walls of the city.

In its palmy days it was called "El-Sherif, the Noble," and even yet the natives cherish its memory, fondly calling it "Merv, the king of the world."

It might be added that the buildings, being

OLD WALLS AROUND ANCIENT CITY OF MERV

mainly constructed of brick, not of a very firm consistency, were not well calculated to resist either the destructive efforts of man or the corroding effects of time.

Alexander the Great is accredited with having founded the ancient city of Merv, which, after

OLD WALL AND GATEWAY IN CITY OF MERV

many vicissitudes through good and ill fortune, was at last almost destroyed in more modern times by Zinghiz Khan, on which occasion it is said over 700,000 of its inhabitants were slaughtered. Tamerlane infused into it some spirit of revival, when it again fell into decline and finally received its "coup de grace" at the hands of an Usbeg conqueror, who cut the canals of the upper Murgab that irrigated the oasis and watered the city, with a result as immediate and disastrous as would follow the severing of the main artery of the human body.

XXI

At Bairom-Ali—Imperial palace—From fertile fields to burning sands—March of Alexander through the desert—From sterile sands to fruitful fields—The Amu-Daria River—Its length, etc.—Quantity of water in the Amu-Daria—Great railway bridge being erected over the Amu-Daria—Possible diversion of the course of this great river—The slow and vast operations of nature—Immense deposits of this great river—Karakul—Rearing of the sheep here known as Persian lamb.

At Bairom-Ali—named after the last defender of Merv—we were received with rare grace and hospitality, and were sumptuously entertained by Colonel de Kaschtalinsky, the imperial agent there, who is directing the important work in progress at that place. Although a small station only, for some reason it has been selected as the site of a superb palace for the future use of the Czar, which is rapidly approaching completion. Extensive gardens and parks are being elaborately laid out around the palace, that will be of surpassing beauty when completed.

After leaving Bairom-Ali, the train for several hours passes though fertile and highly cultivated fields, when it suddenly plunges into a desert that

ACROSS THE DESERT

ACROSS THE BURNING DESERT   451

extends nearly 150 miles. The scene is one of the wildest and most oppressive desolation. It is nothing but an immense sea of the purest sand,

STATION AT BAIROM-ALI ON TRANS-CASPIAN RAILWAY, ON THE ROAD TO BOKHARA

that by the action of the wind is heaped into great ridges and dunes fully 20 to 50 feet high. Wave upon wave and billow upon billow seemed to roll in this vast ocean of sand, in towering heights, one above the other, from the summits of which great clouds were driven like the spray from the crest of a wave in a stormy sea. Every now and again

BUNDLES OF FAGOTS USED AS A SAND BARRIER TO PROTECT THE RAILWAY AGAINST THE DRIFTING SAND

fierce whirls and gusts of sand swept in blinding drifts over the train, which, with the stifling heat, had a most suffocating effect.

Scarcely a vestige of vegetation exists through

.this long and dreary waste; the flight of a solitary bird or the sight of a lone shrub in the distance only emphasized the horrible desolation. The rail-

MARKET SCENE IN THE TOWN OF AMU-DARIA, ON THE BANKS OF THE AMU-DARIA RIVER

way has in many places barriers and guards against the drifting sand, such as are used in winter in other countries against drifting snow.

It was right through these burning sands that

the intrepid Macedonian led his Grecian hosts on his march from Merv to Samarkand and the Trans-Oxian country. It is small wonder that his faithful and obedient soldiers, after following him for years in his career of conquest over Arabian and Persian deserts, Bactrian sands and Himalayan snows, should at last, in the fertile valleys of Northern India, spontaneously throw down their arms and stubbornly refuse to follow their insatiable leader further. Perhaps this it was that caused the monarch to weep, and not, as the sentimental historian puts it, for " more worlds to conquer," as he had just entered upon the verge of the greatest world of all.

The magician's art can scarcely produce an effect more startling than that which followed our sudden transition from the desert, with its torrid heat and blinding sands, to the cool shady groves, the lovely gardens and smiling landscapes in the charming valley of the Amu-Daria. So abrupt was the change that it seemed the work of enchantment.

Amu-Daria, the town located on the banks of the great river of that name, is purely the product of the railway, and, like all Russian towns in this land of exuberant vegetation, the territory it covers is quite disproportionate to its population. Although containing over 20,000 inhabitants and being the centre of an extensive trade, it is more an assemblage of lovely gardens, groves, and parks than a city. The mighty river here, known to the Greeks as the Oxus and so celebrated in their annals, deserves, on account of its great size and many peculiarities, especial mention.

ON THE AMU-DARIA, ABOVE THE CITY OF THAT NAME

It has its source in the lofty mountains of Afghanistan and the Hindu Kush, flowing northward through a distance of 1,200 to 1,500 miles into the Aral Sea, and therefore has no outlet to the ocean. Although its length is but little greater than that of the Danube, it is said that its volume of water is three times as great. Its width at the point where the railway crosses it is quite equal to the average of the Mississippi River between Memphis and Vicksburg. The extraordinary quantity of water that flows in a river of a length so moderate is accounted for by the fact that it has its origin in the highest mountain range in the world, on whose summit the heavily saturated air from the Indian Ocean pours its mighty floods, which descend in the Amu-Daria to the north, and in the Indus and Ganges southward.

The railway bridge is over four versts, or nearly three miles, in length. It is a modern structure built on piles driven into the loose and shifting bed of the river. The government is actively preparing to build an immense iron structure, which is estimated to cost about 18,000,000 rubles, or over $9,000,000.

As the bed of the river is only about twenty-five feet below the level of the surrounding country, and as its channel lies scarcely ten miles from the edge where the descent into Turcomania sharply begins, the diversion of this river into that country is regarded by engineers as a feasible enterprise. The cutting of a canal twenty-five to thirty feet deep, and fifteen to twenty miles long, would be sufficient to form an initial channel through which, in the loose alluvial soil and sands, the river might

TEMPORARY RAILWAY BRIDGE OVER THE AMU-DARIA RIVER

ultimately cut its way and return again to its ancient course to the Caspian Sea.

In this connection, as illustrating the slow processes of nature when on a colossal scale, I

STREET IN AMU-DARIA

would say that it is estimated that it would require over twenty-five years for the waters of this river to reach the Caspian Sea if its full volume were suddenly turned in that direction, so great would be the requirements to supply the loss by evaporation, the needs of the thirsty soil, and to fill the many depressions in the vast intermediate country.

RAILWAY STATION AT THE NEW, OR RUSSIAN, TOWN OF BOKHARA, THE OLD CITY BEING TWELVE MILES FROM THE RAILWAY

The river at the point where the railway crosses it is divided into two channels at low water, each a little over a mile in width. At its full stage, the river extends for three miles from shore to shore. The average volume of water is estimated at about 4,000 cubic meters per second, and it is said to contain nearly two per cent. of earthy matter, mainly suspended clay.

It will be seen, therefore, that this mighty river, since the time Alexander floated his army across it on inflated goat skins, has carried northward nearly 2,000 cubic miles of solid matter, enough to cover the whole State of Ohio to a depth of over 200 feet, and a quantity quite equal to the cubic contents of the Alleghanies in the State of Pennsylvania.

The operation of causes so vast is not without its adequate effects, for the Aral Sea is already 200 feet above the level of the Caspian, and in future may be so lifted that its waters will overflow and find their way again to that sea. The eye of imagination may even discern that in future eons the Caspian itself, and even the great basin of which it is the centre, may yet be filled by the washings of the mountains a thousand miles away. The contemplation of cosmic changes so vast, wrought by the erosions of time, suggesting the ultimate removal of the earth's inequalities, teaches anew the lesson that all things seem to be travelling toward a final, and perhaps an eternal, equilibrium.

After leaving Amu-Daria, the first station

reached is Karakul, which, although a small town, deserves especial mention, as from here and the surrounding region comes most of what is known and so properly prized by the American ladies

NEW PALACE BEING BUILT BY RUSSIA FOR THE AMEER OF BOKHARA, NEAR THE STATION IN THE NEW, OR RUSSIAN, TOWN OF THAT NAME

as Astrakhan, or Persian lamb. The term Astrakhan is a pure misnomer, since none of these animals are reared in that locality. The name Astrakhan as applied to this commodity no doubt grew out of the fact that, owing to the favorable commercial position of that city at the head of the Caspian Sea, it was through Astrakhan that this

OLD MOSQUE SAID TO HAVE BEEN BUILT BY TAMERLANE

highly prized article of dress was first introduced into the West.

It is obtained from a peculiar variety of sheep. It is an under-sized and scraggy animal, in striking contrast with the large, plump, and well-rounded kind that yields the excellent mutton of Bokhara. They are almost without exception black, and it is about as rare to find a white or light one in the flock as is the traditional black sheep in the com-

SUMMER PALACE OF THE AMEER OF BOKHARA, BETWEEN THE NEW AND OLD CITIES OF THAT NAME.

mon variety. Its wool, instead of being long and straight of fibre, grows in short, crisp curls close to the body, and is of exceptionally fine texture. The quality depends almost entirely upon the age at which the animal is killed—the younger it is, the higher the grade.

The very highest quality is produced by a most singular practice. As soon as the lamb is able to stand on its legs, its little body is tightly sewn up in a cloth envelope, in which it is permitted to run about for four or five days, when it is killed. The purpose of this seems to be threefold—to preserve the exquisite lustre and texture of its baby wool, to protect it against being soiled, and to add to the length of the fibre by a few days' growth, as well as more firmly fixing the curl.

It is called here, in the East, Karakul, taking its name from the town and region where it is so extensively produced. It is not valued in the West only, but throughout Central Asia is held in quite as high esteem, every one whose means will bring it within their reach using it in some form. As a sort of guide to its value, I would say that the skins of the best quality sell where it is grown at $4 to $8 apiece.

XXII

Bokhara—Courtesy of Russian officials—The Ameer of Bokhara—Area and population of Bokhara—Its destruction by the Tartars—The ruling race—The Usbegs inferior to the Turcomans—Mosques and colleges—The mosque of Tamerlane in the Reghistan—Inferior to the ruins of Samarkand—Palace of the Ameer of Bokhara—Citadel of Alp-Arslan—Bazaars in Bokhara—Buildings, etc.—Customs, police regulations, etc.—Vices and virtues of the Bokharians—Temperance among the inhabitants—An agreeable contrast—Introduction of opium into Central Asia—An instructive incident.

On my arrival at the new city of Bokhara I was met by the military agent there, who at once assigned us a gighiti, or escort, to the old city, twelve miles away. Bokhara, while nominally an independent khanate, is in reality under Russian control, the Ameer being scarcely more than a vassal of the Czar. The government has but few soldiers in this province, and seems to studiously avoid any display of authority or sovereignty, abstaining from all acts that might be interpreted as pressing or coercive.

It moreover in nowise interferes with the habits and customs of the people. Steady and silent absorption is relied upon to do the work of assimi-

THE AMEER OF BOKHARA

TOWER FORMERLY USED TO EXECUTE CRIMINALS BY THROWING THEM FROM THE TOP

THE AMEER OF BOKHARA 471

lation. No doubt to ingratiate themselves into the graces of the present ruler, the Russians are building a splendid palace for his use at New Bokhara, near the railway station. The Ameer seems

REGHISTAN, OR MARKET-PLACE, IN BOKHARA, NEAR THE OLD CITADEL.

to submit with an amiable docility to the new powers-that-be, and it is said that he is never so well pleased as when he is rigged out in the full dress and trappings of a Russian general.

The province of Bokhara contains over 100,000 square miles, and about 5,000,000 people. It is one of the most fertile on the globe, and is irrigated almost throughout. The Zerafshan River, a tributary of the Amu-Daria, is diverted near

OLD MOSQUE, COVERED WITH VARIEGATED TILES

Samarkand, and its waters carried in large canals to the city of Bokhara, nearly 200 miles, irrigating in the meanwhile the adjacent lands through which they pass. Excepting the Nile valley, in no country, perhaps, are the supreme conditions of agriculture so completely under the control of

BAZAAR IN BOKHARA

VEGETABLE PRODUCTIONS 475

man, or are nature's choicest gifts through the soil so easily obtainable.

Vegetables and fruits grow here in the most surprising profusion and abundance. Grapes of a

A GRAVEYARD IN THE CITY OF BOKHARA

size and quality nowhere surpassed, or scarcely equalled, sell here at less than a cent per pound. Rich pasturage sustains countless herds of sheep that yield meats of the highest quality.

The old city of Bokhara is one of the most peculiar, and even unique, in the world. It contains about 150,000 inhabitants, and is surrounded by a massive wall, in which there are twelve gates that enter the city. It is a very ancient city, and, like Merv, suffered at the hands of the Tartar invader, and was burned in the thirteenth century by Zinghiz Khan. The ruling race are the Usbeg Tartars. They are tillers of the soil, and live largely in cities. Reflecting in many ways the enervating influence of a luxurious life, they are physically far inferior to their nomadic neighbor, the Turcoman.

Excepting Mecca, Bokhara is, perhaps, the centre of the purest Moslem faith in the Mohammedan world. There are about 300 mosques in the city, and in addition about thirty Medressehs, or colleges, to educate the faithful. Some of the mosques are models of beauty, especially that built by Tamerlane, in the Reghistan, or market-place, in front of the palace. Generally, however, they are inferior, both in design and ornamentation, to the splendid ruins of Samarkand.

The palace of the Ameer is located on an eminence near the western limit of the city. Neither in its exterior or interior is it sufficiently striking to command especial attention. It, however, derives interest from the fact that it was built over 1,000

NATIVE BOKHARIANS, FATHER AND SONS

years ago by Alp-Arslan, the great Persian king who so long and gallantly contested with the Eastern Empire of Rome the mastery of the East.

THE CITADEL IN BOKHARA, SAID TO HAVE BEEN BUILT BY ALP-ARSLAN, THE PERSIAN KING. IT IS WITHIN THIS CITADEL THAT THE PALACE OF THE AMEER IS LOCATED

Bokhara has large and important bazaars, but as machine-made goods are rapidly supplanting the more splendid products of the hand, they are fast losing their interest. The buildings are low, seldom of more than two stories, and built with the flat roof so common in Oriental countries. The streets are narrow, and, as they are covered in the

MUEZZIN CALLING THE FAITHFUL TO PRAYER FROM THE MINARET OF A MOSQUE IN BOKHARA

centre or business portion of the town, it is possible to easily walk on the roofs of the houses over a large part of the city.

There are many strange customs and regula-

VIEW OVER THE ROOFS OF THE HOUSES IN BOKHARA

tions here. Every gate leading into the town is closed at evening prayers, and no one is permitted thereafter to enter or depart until after morning prayers, some little time before sunrise. More-

BAZAAR IN BOKHARA

over, at the same hour even the streets are cleared, and no one is allowed to appear upon them during the night. To enforce this regulation, a policeman is stationed every few hundred feet, and, besides, a special detail of watchmen walk over the roofs of the houses throughout the entire night, beating a lively tattoo on their drums. The effect of this is to confine every citizen to his home, and the streets are thus absolutely deserted.

STREET AND OLD MOSQUE IN THE NEIGHBORHOOD OF THE REGHISTAN, OR MARKET-PLACE.

One thing is certain, that life and property are thereby made secure in this queer city.

While there are no doubt many vices here, the city is justly entitled to have many virtues recorded

RUINED MINARET, ENCASED WITH BEAUTIFUL VARIEGATED TILES

to its credit. I was told by the keeper of the caravansary at which we stopped, that theft is almost unknown. He said he had been in the city for ten years, during which time not a single case

RUINS OF ANCIENT MOSQUE NEAR THE REGHISTAN, IN BOKHARA

had come to his notice. As the Mohammedan is not only theoretically, but de facto, an absolute teetotaller, the use and sale of alcoholic liquors of all kinds, even beer and wine, are rigidly prohibited. After having witnessed the wretched and debasing effects of the unrestrained use of intoxicating drinks among nations laying claim to a high civilization, this splendid example of sobriety by a

IRRIGATING CANALS ON THE PLAINS OF BOKHARA, ON THE ROAD TO SAMARKAND. WATER DRAWN FROM THE ZERAFSHAN RIVER

so-called heathen nation was, to say the least, refreshing.

At this point I cannot forbear relating an incident that occurred at Merv, bearing directly upon

the great question as to the future condition of the Oriental races when brought under the influence and power of the Western nations, as doubtless they ultimately will be.

While in that city, I was invited to a dinner given by a Russian high in authority, at which there were several other officials, both civil and military, as well as a number of resident business men. During the evening, the conversation turned upon the material resources and probable industrial development of Russia's Central Asian possessions, which led our host to refer to an interesting circumstance.

A year or so before, an Englishman with important business connections, who was making a tour in that region, was a guest at a dinner given by this same official. The usual discussion naturally arising as to the future trade possibilities of Central Asia, his guest, he said, took occasion to suggest that it might be a profitable business venture for Russia to introduce the opium traffic into that great country.

Having in mind, evidently, the demoralizing results produced by England's forcible introduction of opium into China, the condemnation of this proposal, expressed by the Russian official, was severe in the extreme.

I shall never forget his look of scorn and contempt as he referred to what he called so extraordinary a proposition, that, for the sake of mere sordid gain, they should follow the example set in

COLLEGE, OR MEDRESSEH, IN BOKHARA

China, and introduce this baneful drug, with its pernicious consequences, among the gentle, industrious, and temperate races under their care and control in Central Asia.

XXIII

Bokhara to Samarkand—Residence of Governor of Turkestan—His great civility—Beauty of Samarkand—Avenues of acacias and poplars—The old city of Samarkand—In ruins, but picturesque—Once a great capital—Splendor under the Arabs and under Tamerlane—A seat of learning—Architecture in old city of Samarkand—Colleges in Samarkand—Mosques, tombs, and palaces—The Shah-Zindah—The Tilla-Kari and Khanym—Exquisite effect of tessellated tiles—The great mosque erected by sister of Tamerlane—Similarity of architecture between Central Asia and that of the Moguls in India—A huge pulpit and voluminous Koran.

LEAVING Bokhara in the evening, we arrived at Samarkand in the forenoon of the next day. We went direct to the palace of the Governor of Turkestan, and were received with that polite attention so characteristic of all, and especially of the higher, Russian officials. The residence of the governor is a handsome structure, nestled in the midst of a most beautiful garden and park, and is furnished throughout with the choicest products of Eastern art.

On making known our wishes we were promptly assigned an escort, whose duty it was to constantly attend us in and about the city during our stay.

We were also informed that the military agent would be ready to respond to our wishes. Although Tashkent, in virtue of its being nearer the centre of Turkestan, is to become the future cap-

PARK IN THE CITY OF SAMARKAND, IN FRONT OF THE TOMB OF TAMERLANE.

ital of this great province, for the present its affairs are conducted from Samarkand.

There are, perhaps, few cities in the world that will at all compare with the rare and peculiar beauty

STREET SCENE IN SAMARKAND

of the new, or Russian, Samarkand. It presents the appearance of having been literally carved out of a dense forest of poplars and acacias, many square

MOSQUE NEAR THE REGHISTAN, AND BUILT BY TAMERLANE, IN SAMARKAND

miles in extent. The tall trees, whose branches almost interlace overhead, form streets of exceptional width, and, crossing at right angles, they form hollow squares, in the centre of which the residences and even business houses are located. In fact, a more perfect sylvan city would be hard to imagine. Along both sides of the streets are

MOSQUE NEAR CENTRE OF CITY, BUILT BY TAMERLANE, CALLED THE TILLA-KARI

running streams of pure, clear water, drawn from the mountains some miles away.

Like many other unfortunate cities whose wealth and splendor caused them to become the prey of

STREET SCENE IN SAMARKAND

the despoiler, and which, through centuries of misfortune and ever-changing masters, descended at last to a fixed state of hopeless despair, the old city of Samarkand, located at some distance from

STREET SCENE IN SAMARKAND, SHOWING THE MOSQUE OF KHANYM, ERECTED BY TAMERLANE TO HIS FAVORITE WIFE, A CHINESE PRINCESS

the new, is now scarcely more than a suggestion of its former greatness. Its streets are narrow and unclean; its houses small and untidy; and the great structures that were once its pride lie scattered about, many in mouldering ruins, and most of them in the last stages of decay; all of them,

STREET SCENE IN SAMARKAND.

however, present an interesting and picturesque appearance.

There is, perhaps, no city in the world that contains so many, or such a variety of, splendid ruins as this. It was known to the ancients as Mara-

MOHAMMEDANS AT PRAYER

canda, and was used by Alexander as a base for his military operations in Sogdiana. It rose to great eminence in the tenth century, and then fell under

ENTRANCE TO THE MOSQUE SHAH-ZINDAH. TESSELLATED TILES, WITH VARIEGATED COLORING.

the hand of that merciless destroyer of nations, Zinghiz Khan. After the mighty Tamerlane ascended the throne of Zagatai, he made Samarkand his capital, and by his efforts it became a brilliant centre of art, refinement, and learning, that, under this ruler and his successors, long shone as the brightest star in the Asiatic firmament.

The genius of Tamerlane can be seen everywhere reflected in the architecture and art of this city and the surrounding country. Many of the finest mosques and colleges are his creation, notably the Tilla-Kari and the Khanym, the latter erected in honor of his favorite wife, who was a Chinese princess. Some of the chief buildings, which are fairly well-preserved, and the mosques whose domes, façades, and minarets are yet covered with tessellated tiles, of those enchanting blues and other colors so in favor with the Persian and Saracen—arranged in exquisite and variegated patterns and designs—combine to produce an indescribably charming effect.

What was perhaps the largest, and generally esteemed one of the most beautiful, mosques in the Mohammedan world, is the Shah-Zindah, just outside of the present, and which once must have been in the midst of the old, city. The memorial mosque, however, built by Tamerlane's sister, when in its best estate, must have been without a peer in the world's rare creations of architecture. It is still sufficiently well-preserved to enable the imagination to restore it in its wondrous pristine symmetry and peerless beauty.

MEDRESSEH, OR NATIVE COLLEGE, IN OLD SAMARKAND

Indeed, to my mind there is but one building in the world that can justly rank as a rival, and that is the memorial mosque erected in India by the Mogul ruler Shah-Jehan to his favorite wife, the Taj-Mahal. To all who are familiar with the art

STREET SCENE IN SAMARKAND. STREET LEADING FROM RAILWAY STATION TO THE CITADEL IN THE CITY

that developed under the Tartar dynasty of Northwestern India, a similarity is apparent so striking as to suggest that it received its inspiration from Central Asia. It is said, in fact, that the architect who designed the Taj-Mahal came from the latter country. As it is a matter of history that the

Tartar ancestors of those who founded the Mogul Empire in India came originally from Central Asia, it is a reasonable supposition that its art also may have been transplanted to the former country.

RUINS OF THE MOSQUE BUILT BY SISTER OF TAMERLANE. ONLY A SMALL PORTION OF IT REMAINS IN GOOD STATE OF PRESERVATION

Within a grove in front of this mosque is an immense marble block, supported by six columns. In the upper part of the block a large V-shaped groove is cut, in which was formerly placed a huge

volume of the Koran, from which the officiating priest read lessons to the surrounding multitude. This great book, which is still preserved in the archives of the mosque of Shah-Zindah, has leaves which seem to be from three to four feet wide and four to five feet long.

XXIV

Medressehs or colleges in Samarkand—The tomb of Tamerlane—The sarcophagus of the great Tartar—Interior ornamentation—The Russian citadel—Kok-Tash, or throne of Tamerlane—The Shadman-Melik—Its peculiar construction—Excursion in the mountains—The beauty of Samarkand—Reminiscences of Alexander the Great—Social customs, etc.—Polygamy—Peculiar equipage.

There are ten or a dozen Medressehs, or native colleges, here, some of them accommodating many hundreds of students. The buildings are two or three stories high, enclosing a quadrangular space, in which also the students live, and thus they much resemble the colleges of English universities. At one side there is invariably located a mosque for the use of the college.

The Gur-Amir, or tomb of Tamerlane here, is worthy of that mighty conqueror. It is of the usual mosque form, and surmounted by a high and ornate dome. In the centre of an octagonal-shaped room, immediately beneath the dome, is placed the sarcophagus containing the remains of this great warrior. It is a huge block of solid jasper, highly

INTERIOR OF TAMERLANE'S TOMB. HIS SARCOPHAGUS AND THOSE OF HIS SON AND PRIME MINISTER

THE TOMB OF TAMERLANE

polished and covered with Cufic inscriptions. On each side is a large porphyry sarcophagus, containing respectively the remains of his son and prime

STREET SCENE IN THE NEW, OR RUSSIAN, CITY OF SAMARKAND

minister. The whole room, as well as the ceiling of the dome, is richly colored and covered with ornamental arabesque fret-work. Through beautifully stained glass windows the light is admitted and diffused through the room in soft, delicate tints.

The old palace is located in what is now a Rus-

TOMB OF TAMERLANE, LOCATED ON THE EDGE OF A GREAT PARK IN THE NEW, OR RUSSIAN, CITY OF SAMARKAND

sian citadel. It contained the celebrated Kok-Tash, or throne of Tamerlane, which was situated in what once was the audience hall of that king. It is a square block of polished jasper of some ten

KOK-TASH, OR THRONE OF TAMERLANE.

feet in length, and, like the sarcophagus, is covered with inscriptions in Cufic letters.

About twelve miles distant from the city are the remains of an ancient bridge, the construction of

ENTRANCE TO THE TOMB OF TAMERLANE

which is accredited to Tamerlane, called the Shadman-Malik. It was thrown across the Zerafshan River, which here spreads over the valley in many channels or branches. The bridge must, therefore, have been an immense structure, and built in a series of great arches. Only one remains intact, although the partial remains of many are yet easily traceable. They were constructed of brick, and I should judge were nearly 100 feet span, and

EXTERIOR OF TOMB OF TAMERLANE, IN NEW, OR RUSSIAN, CITY OF SAMARKAND

of a height of sixty to eighty feet. For some unaccountable reason the arches did not extend in a straight line, but were all placed at an angle to each other, giving to the long structure a zigzag course.

THE SHADMAN-MALIK, OR BRIDGE OF TAMERLANE

We made a pleasant excursion into the hills and low range of mountains to the northeast of the city. While affording many charming views and much picturesque scenery, this region derives especial interest from the fact that it was here Alex-

STREET SCENE IN SAMARKAND

ander received a dangerous wound, and sustained his first, and perhaps only, reverse, at the hands of the fierce hill tribes of this locality. If history be not at fault, this was not the only wound received here by this dauntless warrior, for he also fell a victim to the charms of the fair Roxana, the daughter of a mountain chieftain, whom he afterwards made his queen.

BURIAL PLACE OF MOHAMMEDAN SAINTS, NEAR THE GREAT MOSQUE OF THE TILLA-KARI, IN SAMARKAND.

There are many social customs and peculiarities here that lend a varied interest to the city. Polygamy still prevails and wives abound, the number

A QUEER EQUIPAGE. A MOHAMMEDAN AND HIS WIVES OUT FOR A DRIVE

A MOHAMMEDAN FAMILY

that a man takes unto himself being limited, as in other Mohammedan countries, by his means to support them. It is no uncommon sight to see a native cart, with its huge wheels and one horse, passing slowly down the shady streets, the rider—

MARKET SCENE IN SAMARKAND

it has no driver—richly dressed, wearing an immense turban, and perched on the very shoulders of the horse to guide the vehicle, on the floor of which, closely veiled, can be seen a number of women, often a half dozen. Having so frequently observed this peculiar outfit, I was moved to inquire the real nature of so strange an equipage, and was informed that it was the custom of wealthy men thus to take their wives out for an airing.

XXV

Natives, or Sarts—Seeing native life and customs—Dinner at the residence of the Amban or native mayor of Samarkand—Our host and his guests—Oriental features of the occasion—Brilliant surroundings—The Russians—The dances—No women as dancers—Boy dancers dressed in the habits of women—The music of the Sart—At first unpleasant—Wherein lies the charm of Oriental music—Due to rhythm—Influence hypnotic—Similar emotional state of howling and dancing dervishes—The dinner—Various native dishes—Kisbab—Cavourna—Pilaf, etc.—Oriental dancing—Producing similar effects by rhythm of motion—Concluding reflections.

This region is peopled by a peculiar race called Sarts who, in many of their traits, seem to be midway between the Chinese and the Tartar, being, as it is said, next to the Chinaman, the most skilful agriculturists in the world. Having expressed a desire to see their domestic life in its primitive and characteristic forms, the governor most obligingly instructed the Amban, or mayor, of the old city to provide for us a dinner and entertainment that would reflect the chief habits and customs of the people. It was arranged to take place at the residence of that official, who was himself a native of great wealth and influence.

On our arrival at the appointed hour, we found

already assembled a large number of guests, all natives and friends of our host, and, from their appearance, wealthy and influential citizens. The

A MOHAMMEDAN AND HIS WIVES. SCENE IN THE PARK IN THE NEW, OR RUSSIAN, CITY OF SAMARKAND.

residence was purely Oriental in design, construction, and ornamentation, the Persian element entering largely into it—a preference I had often before observed shown by these people. It was two stories in height, enclosing an open court of perhaps eighty feet square, entirely covered for the occasion by large rugs, rich in brilliant colorings and tasteful patterns. The owner, with his

NATIVES, OR SARTS, FATHER AND SON

family, occupied the front and two sides of the building, the rear one being reserved for the domestics.

The dining table was located on a sort of wide

veranda or dais running around the interior of the building at some height from the ground, from which we looked directly upon the court below; at

MEDRESSEH, OR NATIVE COLLEGE, LOCATED IN THE OLD CITY OF SAMARKAND. THERE ARE SAID TO BE SOME TWENTY COLLEGES IN SAMARKAND

the opposite side of the court the musicians, some ten or twelve in number, as is the custom of the country, sat squatting on the carpets. The table accommodated about thirty guests, and, excepting two Russian soldiers in full military dress, detailed by the government for this function, there were no

STREET SCENE IN THE OLD CITY OF SAMARKAND, LEADING FROM THE PUBLIC SQUARE TO THE GREAT MOSQUE OF TAMERLANE.

foreigners other than ourselves. There were no women present, as they are, in fact, rarely seen on any public occasion.

In addition to the musicians, there was provided

for our entertainment a full corps of professional dancers, composed of youths from fifteen to eighteen years of age, and dressed as girls—no women,

IN THE OLD CITY OF SAMARKAND. STREET LEADING TO THE GREAT MOSQUE OF THE SHAH-ZINDAH. NATIVE SARTS IN THE FOREGROUND.

as is the custom throughout the East, being permitted to publicly appear in any kind of theatrical representation. The instruments were the usual flat drum, a sort of clarionet, and cymbals. Immediately after the beginning of the dinner, the music commenced, and continued, with only short intervals, during the entire repast. The highly-pitched voices of the singers, mingled with what at first seemed the discordant din of the instruments,

STREET SCENE IN THE RUSSIAN, OR NEW, CITY OF SAMARKAND

produced anything but a pleasant effect. Such is the inscrutable law of adjustment, however, that after being under its influence for several hours, not only did it cease to be unpleasant, but

I even began to discover elements of beauty and pleasure in it.

I wish I were sufficiently versed in music to make an effort to determine wherein lies the charm of the music of the East, since it certainly

RUINS OF THE MOSQUE OF THE SHAH-ZINDAH, IN THE OLD CITY OF SAMARKAND, SAID TO HAVE BEEN ONE OF THE GRANDEST IN THE MOSLEM WORLD

has a decided charm for the Oriental ear, as they always listen to it in a dreamy silence. I am inclined to think that it is due to its rhythm, producing a sort of hypnotic spell upon the hearer. To the influence of rhythm is evidently due that strange entrancement displayed by the dancing and howling dervishes of the East, and the somewhat similar mental and emotional state shown by the negro in America on certain occasions of high religious excitement.

ENTRANCE THROUGH THE ENCLOSING WALL THAT SURROUNDS THE TOMB OF TAMERLANE, IN THE CITY OF SAMARKAND

The strange effect of adjustment was exemplified by a circumstance that occurred while on a visit to Japan some years ago. I fell in with a highly intelligent Japanese gentleman, who had returned a few months before from England, where he had spent fifteen years, and had graduated at one of its leading universities. He had been sufficiently long in the West to become familiar with its customs, and had, as he said, acquired some fondness for its music. I asked him which

VIEW IN THE PARK IN THE OLD CITY OF SAMARKAND

he preferred, when he freely admitted that he liked best the simple music of his own country, which to me was almost painful.

The viands served by our host were entirely those of the natives. The first dish was called Kiabab, made of minced meat, previously cooked

DANCERS AND MUSICIANS AT BANQUET IN SAMARKAND

and deliciously flavored, wrapped in successive layers of a thin sheet of dough, forming small rolls, and dropped into some sort of hot fat and browned. The second dish was called Cavourna,

NATIVE MUSICIANS IN THE OLD CITY OF SAMARKAND

and was a kind of meat stew, made of mutton and various vegetables, such as tomatoes, etc.

The great dish, however, the *pièce de résistance*, was Pilaf, which, like the curry of India, is the main article of diet in the Central East. It is made by mixing choice bits of fried mutton with boiled rice, to which is added something like curry.

It constitutes a palatable and withal a most digestible and wholesome dish. The last course was fruits, the variety and excellence of which I will not attempt to describe. Although wines of many choice varieties, produced by the resident

DANCERS AT BANQUET IN THE OLD CITY OF SAMARKAND

Russians, were liberally served. I noticed that not one of the guests—all being Mohammedans—touched it, not even to respond to a toast.

The dancing was of a variety so universally in

vogue throughout Oriental countries. It is in its nature essentially allied to their music, a like effect being produced in both instances by the same primary cause—rhythm—acting in the one case through the ear, in the other through the eye.

SHADMAN-MALIK, OR BRIDGE OF TAMERLANE, OVER THE ZERAFSHAN RIVER, TWENTY MILES FROM CITY OF SAMARKAND

What is accomplished by the almost monotonous repetition of rhythmic sounds, is done quite as effectively by the continuous repetition of gentle and graceful movements of the limbs and the body. The combined effect, therefore, of their music and dancing is to lull those who are accustomed to it into a drowsy, dreamy mood. Occasionally a dancer would suddenly break away from the rest and, in rapid gyrations and dizzy whirls, spin around in a great circle, his long, loose hair

MARKET SCENE IN THE OLD CITY OF SAMARKAND

and flowing robe in the meanwhile circling in the air with curious effect.

At different intervals a magician, juggler, or acrobat was called in to lend additional interest to the entertainment. So absorbed was I in all that was occurring that I took no note of time, and on suddenly discovering that more than three hours had been consumed, I at once signified to my host that I must depart. Amid many profound salaams, and a profusion of good wishes for our welfare and safety, we took our departure from scenes and experiences that I shall always remember as the most weird and interesting of my life.

STREET SCENE IN THE NEW TOWN OF SAMARKAND

While returning, I pondered much on the inscrutable causes that operate to create nations, and to control their destinies. How strange it seemed that, by the influence of what appear to be the same causes and similar natural laws in different regions of the globe, there are created races so widely divergent in customs, habits, and modes of thought, and even in physical characteristics. More wonderful still is it, that a sudden and violent change from the fixed conditions of one nation to those of another is often followed by national and even racial death.

Perhaps we may find a partial solution of these mysteries in the fact that what we are accustomed superficially to regard as identical or similar conditions may, upon a closer analysis, prove to be widely different in essential particulars; and, therefore, whatever peculiar traits a nation may display will be found to be only the natural and necessary outgrowth of the special conditions under which it evolved.

These reflections would seem to harmonize with what a great philosopher has declared to be the general law of life—"the adjustment of internal to external relations." They also tend to carry us closer toward the inquiry, whether our thoughts, customs, tastes, and even our physical being may not be merely the continuous product of the environing conditions in which, and by which, we exist.

THE END.

www.ingramcontent.com/pod-product-compliance
Lightning Source LLC
Chambersburg PA
CBHW031936290426
44108CB00011B/574